A Practitioners' Tool for the Assessment of Adults who Sexually Abuse Children

Jeff Fowler

Jessica Kingsley Publishers
London and Philadelphia

First published in 2008
by Jessica Kingsley Publishers
116 Pentonville Road
London N1 9JB, UK
and
400 Market Street, Suite 400
Philadelphia, PA 19106, USA
www.jkp.com

Library of Congress Cataloging in Publication Data

Fowler, Jeff, 1947-
    A practitioners' tool for the assessment of adults who sexually abuse children / Jeff
Fowler.
        p. ; cm.
    Includes bibliographical references.
    ISBN 978-1-84310-639-5 (pb : alk. paper) 1. Child sexual abuse--Diagnosis. 2.
Child molesters--Identification. I. Title.
    [DNLM: 1. Child Abuse, Sexual--diagnosis. 2. Adult. 3. Pedophilia--diagnosis. WM
610 F786p 2008]
    RC560.C46F69 2008
    616.85'8369075--dc22
                                                                    2007038503

British Library Cataloguing in Publication Data
A CIP catalogue record for this book is available from the British Library

ISBN 978 1 84310 639 5

Printed and bound in Great Britain by
Athenaeum Press, Gateshead, Tyne and Wear

CONTENTS

ACKNOWLEDGEMENTS

To all those who have shared their knowledge and expertise over the years.

To all those whose experiences of being sexually abused have been shared through assessment or therapy.

To Sheila Fowler, whose comments added greatly to this book.

INTRODUCTION

This practitioner's tool is designed to be used in child protection assessments and for training purposes. It does not explore the theories which underpin the understanding of adults who sexually abuse children. It is however essential that practitioners using this book are familiar with those theories and apply their principles in the assessment process.

It is the most difficult kind of child abuse for the majority of people to understand.

It challenges so many of our traditionally held values.

It is something you cannot imagine happening to children.

How can people do this to children?

Sexual abuse destroys a person's whole life.

Men who sexually molest children should be castrated.

I think it is overstated and overestimated.

It's normal in some countries, why not here?

It's part of growing up – it has to happen sooner or later.

These are just a very small sample of the comments made to me over the years about the sexual abuse of children. It is a subject which evokes the most extreme emotions in people. It challenges professionals to develop the following skills and abilities:

- to understand the impact of sexual abuse on children

- to understand what informs and motivates adults to sexually abuse children

- to develop appropriate child protection systems

- to help children survive their experiences

- to help those adults who were sexually abused as children to protect their own children from similar experiences

- to help treat perpetrators.

Many years ago a comment was made to me that sexual abuse is not as bad as other forms of abuse: children who are physically abused or neglected sometimes die, but that is not a consequence of sexual abuse. Following years of experience of assessing adults who were sexually abused as children, I know how flawed that comment was. Children who are sexually abused have their physical and emotional health compromised in a way which, in many cases, affects them throughout their entire adult life. Self-harm, depression, a lack of ability with relationships and unresolved feelings of guilt, shame and anger are in my experience a more common consequence of this type of abuse than any other. Difficulties with child protection, including placing their own children at greater risk of sexual abuse, are also relevant.

Like so much in the field of child protection, the identification of sexual abuse has been a combination of realisation, revolution and evolution. When I first trained in the early 1970s sexual abuse was regarded as neither prevalent nor relevant to my training requirements. However, the incidence of sexual abuse became increasingly apparent through individual cases, professional awareness and some public exposure. At that stage there was no purposeful or co-ordinated response to the assessment or treatment of youngsters who had been victims of sexual abuse. Some initiatives were taken, but we were learning about this form of child abuse at the same time as we were developing strategies to evaluate and respond.

Public opinion was galvanised by people such as Esther Rantzen, the founder of ChildLine, a free telephone service for youngsters who are being abused. Many professionals, including those who were working with at-risk families, were stunned by the extent of the problem. It fuelled a determination to develop a knowledge and skills base to identify and assess situations where children were disclosing sexual abuse. That process remains dynamic. Professionals now have systems in place for protecting children who have suffered or are at risk of suffering significant harm because they are being sexually abused. Child Protection case conferences incorporate sexual abuse within their registration criteria.

Sexual abuse is described in child protection as being the actual or likely sexual exploitation of a child or adolescent. The child may be dependent and/or developmentally immature, does not truly comprehend, or is unable to give informed consent. The abuser may use bribes, threats or physical force to persuade a child or adolescent to participate in sexual activity.

Assessment procedures have been developed through practice, collaboration and learned skills. Each new assessment provides thought and information which might inform a different approach to future assessments or in respect of an individual assessment. As with all assessments which involve people there is no absolute formula which can be applied. There are, however, fundamental principles, structures and systems which enable the assessment of adults who sexually abuse children. The process of assessment must continue to remain dynamic and must be responsive. Children are now more vulnerable to sexual exploitation and sexual abuse than at any time in the past.

This book specifically deals with the assessment of adults who sexually abuse children and the assessment of the non-abusing adult/partner. There is some information in respect of treatment programmes or forms of therapeutic intervention but this is in the form of general information. Such work requires a very different framework of skills and experiences.

This guide provides professionals who work in the area of child protection with a framework to assess adults who sexually abuse children. It enables decisions to be made on the basis of the systematic collection and interpretation of information. It does not provide the theoretical underpinning.

There are a number of different situations and circumstances in which children are sexually abused by adults:

- from within the family group by a parent or step-parent

- by an adult from the extended family group

- by adults well known to the children, for example, family friends and people within organisations and groups

- by people previously unknown to the children who make contact and establish relationships with them for the purpose of grooming them for sexual abuse.

Whilst all of these adults will be considered within the book, the nature of child protection usually focuses on the family, extended family and friendship group as they have an ongoing implication in terms of child protection.

This practitioner's guide looks at the issue of sexual abuse under three distinct headings:

- the child

- the abusing adult

- the non-abusing adult.

SAFEGUARDING CHILDREN

The Children Act 2004, Section 11, places a statutory duty on key people and bodies to make arrangements to safeguard and promote the welfare of children.

In order to do this effectively the concept of 'working together' and 'multi-disciplinary/multi-agency' policy and practice have become enshrined in child protection arrangements. It is essential this is adopted when assessments are completed in cases of child sexual abuse.

Local Safeguarding Children Boards (LSCBs)

Every local authority needs to have in place a Local Safeguarding Children Board and this now forms Chapter 3 of *Working Together to Safeguard Children* (Department of Health 2006).

Within that chapter reference is made to the establishment and effective functioning of Area Child Protection Committees (ACPCs). This is an inter-agency forum which acts as the focal point for local co-operation to safeguard children. It operates from the informing principle that child protection arrangements must involve all professionals and practitioners involved with the child and the family.

Working Together to Safeguard Children (Department of Health 2006)

This 238-page document is a guide to inter-agency working to safeguard and promote the welfare of children. It promotes a range of arrangements which are designed to protect children, which:

depends upon effective working between agencies and professionals that have different roles and expertise. Individual children, especially some of the most vulnerable children and those at greater risk of social exclusion, will need co-ordinated help from health, education, children's social care, and quite possibly the voluntary sector and other agencies.

Joint working

The principle of joint working and collaboration between all professionals involved with any family where children have suffered or are at risk of suffering significant harm through child sexual abuse is crucial to the best interests of children. It should inform and underpin any assessment of adults who have sexually abused children and of the adult who is being assessed as the 'safe adult'.

INTRODUCTION TO THE PRACTITIONER'S TOOL

The purpose of this practitioner's tool is to provide professionals with a systematic way of collecting and interpreting the information which allows for the assessment of adults who sexually abuse children and, where appropriate, the non-abusing adult. Its purpose is to assess the risk which perpetrators present to children and families and to understand the extent to which the non-abusing adult is able to protect the children from the risk of further abuse.

It concentrates on constructing the understanding from a child protection perspective rather than from a forensic or offence perspective, although inevitably there are overlaps and similarities. Therefore an emphasis is placed upon the family unit in which the sexual abuse has occurred and in which the perpetrator lives, would like to live or has recently been a member.

There is a presumption that the workers involved in the assessment are qualified and experienced in child protection, or are being appropriately mentored and supported to undertake such work. The work will often have a multi-disciplinary and multi-agency perspective. Its conclusions will be incorporated into child protection agreements and will inform the future arrangements for the care of the child and the role that the perpetrator may have with the victim and his or her family in the future.

The book incorporates the principles of child protection assessments and can be used alongside the *Framework for the Assessment of Children in Need and their Families* (Department of Health 2000) and *A Practitioner's Tool for Child Protection and the Assessment of Parents* (Fowler 2003). It is designed to construct an understanding of the abusing adult and non-abusing adult, where that is appropriate, in a methodical and systematic fashion. The principle of this assessment is that the behaviour of adults is informed by their childhood and life experiences and the unique way in which those experiences have been internalised. It does not presume that adults who have been sexually abused as children will become abusers in their adult life although it recognises that, unless unhelpful childhood experiences have been resolved either by the person's own resources or with professional help, there is a greater likelihood of perpetrator behaviour occurring.

The checklists are designed to be easily reproduced for use in individual sessions within the assessment. Some of the checklists are for guidance only, and that is the case with all those relating to the background, childhood and adult life experiences of the adults. It is recommended that those checklists which relate specifically to the abusing adult behaviour and the non-abusing adult's ability to protect are used in their entirety as they have been designed to build up the most comprehensive understanding possible.

There has been considerable debate over the years as to the value or otherwise of checklists, and no doubt their use will have supporters and critics both now and in the future. Their value for practitioners is that they permit the issues to be considered and discussed at a level which ensures that all relevant information and detail is collected. They should not, however, prevent the incorporation of subsidiary questions which might arise from individual answers or from an overview of a particular area of discussion.

It is important that practitioners do not simply use the checklists in isolation. Information from other sources, observation from previous sessions and other parts of the assessment should all be incorporated into the overall view which is formed. Practitioners should not merely take the views expressed by those adults being assessed without revisiting, challenging or seeking further clarification. Most adults who are being assessed within child protection are likely to want to present themselves in the best way possible. They are likely to try to reflect themselves in the most positive light, minimise their previous behaviour or risk and may not therefore be entirely truthful in the answers they give. There must, however, always be a balance between being proactive and challenging in seeking an understanding of an adult's behaviour and treating people being assessed with courtesy and dignity.

The book includes a case study which uses the checklists. Notes are produced at the end of each checklist to highlight some of the responses, cross-reference information and indicate the likely areas of concern or positive outcome.

CHAPTER 1

The Child

1.1 THE CHILD

Whilst each child is affected in their own unique way by the abuse they have suffered, it is clear that children who have been sexually abused will have their physical and emotional wellbeing significantly compromised. Where child protection is an issue the child is frequently abused by a trusted adult. Consequently, an adult on whom the child relied to be kept physically safe and emotionally well has breached that trust to such an extent that the child is likely to have felt fearful, abandoned, violated and angry.

Relevant information about child sexual abuse

- Of 250 child victims studied by DeFrancis, 50 per cent experienced physical force, such as being held down, struck, or shaken violently (Becker 1994 as cited in Bolen 2001).

- Studies have not found differences in the prevalence of child sexual abuse among different social classes or races. However, parental inadequacy, unavailability, conflict and a poor parent–child relationship are among the characteristics that distinguish children at risk of being sexually abused (Finklehor 1994).

- According to the *Third National Incidence Study*, girls are sexually abused three times more often than boys, whereas boys are more likely to die or be seriously injured from their abuse (Sedlak and Broadhurst 1996).

- Both boys and girls are most vulnerable to abuse between the ages of 7 and 13 (Finklehor 1994).

- Police Research Series, Paper 99, 'Sex offending against children: Understanding the risk', prepared by Don Grubin, identified the following key points about sex offenders:

  o Judging by the numbers of cases reported to the police, sex offending against children may be even more prevalent than population surveys have indicated previously.

  o The majority of offenders offend in the house and abuse children who are members of their family or are known to them.

  o The consequences of being abused in the home by a known and trusted adult are often more serious than being abused by a stranger.

- o Adolescent offenders probably account for up to a third of sex crimes. Multi-agency work needs to identify and treat more young offenders (and their victims) who are most at risk of continuing to offend.

- o About 20 per cent of those who are convicted of sex offences against children are re-convicted for similar offences; the Rapid Risk Assessment for Sex Offender Recidivism (RRASOR) (Hanson 1997) and Structured Anchored Clinical Judgement (SACJ) (Graham 2000) risk assessment instruments can be used to identify offenders who represent a high risk of re-offending.

- o Multi-agency work is needed to achieve the goal of managing the risk of sex offenders in the community.

The impact of sexual abuse on children

The extent to which children are adversely affected primarily depends upon two issues.

What is sexual abuse?

The sexual abuse of a child is any act which uses or attempts to use a child for the purpose of sexual gratification or in any sexual act. If the child feels he or she is being sexually abused or exploited then from their perspective that is what is happening. Even if the child does not recognise the act as being sexually abusive because of age or lack of understanding, if any intimate part of the child's body is involved, sexual abuse is taking place.

- Such behaviour in adults ranges from inappropriate touching to acts of violent rape.

- The abuse can be a single act or persistent sexual abuse over a lengthy period.

- It can involve a single adult (a private and secret event) or several adults (public abuse containing an element of humiliation).

- The abuse can result in physical injuries and permanent damage to the child's body.

The internalisation of the abuse

Children deal with their abuse in uniquely different ways. Some children who have been inappropriately touched over a brief period may have the most extreme of reactions which persists throughout their adult life. Other children who have been overtly abused over a long period have managed to deal with what has happened to them and get on with their lives. So the severity of the abuse does not determine the extent to which the child's physical and emotional health is compromised.

- Some children are tremendously resilient and survive what has happened to them. They develop 'defence mechanisms' which prevent the abuse from impacting on their lives.

- For some children these defence mechanisms protect them throughout their adult life. Such a system of dealing with abuse is not, however, a solution; it is a management device. Practitioners should not presume that it will never resurface as a problem at some time in the future.

- Others are locked into what has happened to them to an extent that they are unable to move on. Their lives are dominated by the abuse and destroyed by its consequences.

The effect of sexual abuse on children

Physically children can suffer irreversible injuries which cause lifelong pain or remove the ability to have children of their own. In some cultures, where virginity is an essential part of adult relationships and marriage, it can result in ostracism and condemnation in adult life.

Emotionally it can be an experience from which children recover and regain their emotional health, or one which constantly invades their thinking and informs their behaviour. They remain emotionally traumatised in adult life. Self-harm, dysfunctional relationships, emotional and mental ill health are often seen in adults who were sexually abused as children. In some cases adults who were sexually abused as children have children who are themselves sexually abused by adults. There are others who become abusers themselves.

Sexual abuse not only impacts upon the physical and emotional health of children; it involves a level of intimacy and privacy. Whereas physical abuse, emotional abuse and neglect have an overwhelming characteristic of rejection, sexual abuse has a confusing combination of closeness and distance, of love on the one hand and anger, rejection and violence on the other.

In adult life, children who have been sexually abused often deal with the experiences by 'blocking'. This is a defence mechanism whereby the abusive events are prevented from invading the person's current thinking. There is, however, always a danger that a trigger event or thought will resurrect the trauma and the issue once more becomes live. It is almost always the case that adults who were sexually abused as children will benefit from professional help to deal with the abuse and practitioners should always consider such advice.

There are a number of ways in which the abusive behaviour of the adult impacts upon the child.

Self-blame and guilt (internal)

This happens when the child sees themselves as being responsible for what is happening. These children frequently have low self-esteem and poor self-image. Comments which confirm this would include:

'It's my fault, I must be bad.'

'I am to blame.'

'It only happened when I was naughty.'

'I was always flirting with him so it must be my fault.'

'I was the only one he did it to so it must be my fault.'

'It's all I was good for.'

Self-blame and guilt (external)

This occurs when others generate the feelings of blame and guilt. It is usually the abusing adult, but could be the non-abusing adult. It is not unusual, where one child makes a disclosure, for the other parent and/or the remaining sibling group to blame the victim. Fear that the disclosure may disintegrate the family unit, anger, if believing that the victim is lying, and jealousy because of sibling rivalry are all emotions which are frequently seen. Comments may include:

'My mother said I have ruined her life.'

'My dad said if he went to prison it would be my fault and he would kill himself – he did.'

'My sister said I have broken up the whole family – I suppose I have really.'

'Everybody said I gave him the come on.'

Note: Practitioners should not presume that siblings who deny they have been abused or who collaborate in imposing pressure for the victim to withdraw their allegation have not been victims themselves.

Cognitive distortions

Some children distort their thinking at the time of the abuse and subsequently. That of course can make them vulnerable to further abuse and the re-abuse of children is something to which practitioners should always be alert. Comments indicative of such distortions might include:

'It only happened when he was drunk.'

'He only did it because he loved me.'

'Mum had changed for the better – I did not want her to start drinking again.'

It also means they may be less alert and/or less able to protect their own children and may possibly lead to them becoming abusers in the future.
Some children adopt the perpetrator's belief systems:

'Children enjoy sex.'

'The age of consent should be brought down. I was only ten but I knew what I was doing.'

'It's only natural when you love someone so much.'

Other distortions can include:

'I am now damaged goods.'

This can lead to children having no respect for their body and allowing others to abuse them or becoming indiscriminately promiscuous.
In some cases the distorted thinking includes perceived responsibilities:

'I let him abuse me so that he would leave the others alone.'

Fear

Fear often plays a significant part in the sexual abuse of children. Sometimes the fear results from violence within the abusive behaviour; at other times it comes from threats. Comments include:

'He said I would be taken into care and never see my mother again.'

'She said she would kill my brother if I told anyone.'

'He said he would set fire to me if I told anyone.'

Signs and symptoms of sexual abuse

Children respond to being sexually abused in different ways, but generally practitioners should be alert to any changes in presentation and behaviour irrespective of whether they are gradual or sudden. Individual behaviour or emotional indicators should not by themselves be used to make decisions but may signal the need for further exploration or monitoring. Multiple indicators would normally require a more proactive response but any investigation should be planned and subject to an agreed child protection protocol.

Signs of sexual abuse occur in three areas:

Physical signs

- sexually transmitted infections

- soreness of the genital area

- pregnancy

- recurrent urinary infection

- persistent constipation

- self-harming

- self-harming of the genitalia

- unexplained bleeding or discharge

- presence of objects in sexual orifices

- injuries to the genitals or rectum

- bruising in or around the genital area

- bruising indicative of holding, for example holding a child in the prone position

- recurrent abdominal pain.

Emotional signs

- depression
- fear of being alone
- fear of specific adults
- fear of particular places or events
- poor levels of trust
- changed levels of trust in particular adults
- isolation and withdrawal, including solitary play
- emotional restlessness.

Behaviour

- inappropriate behaviour
- sexually inappropriate behaviour
- sudden or gradual changes in behaviour
- sleep disorders
- eating disorders
- school refusal
- running away
- inappropriately adult behaviour
- promiscuous behaviour
- regression, for example a return to more childlike behaviour
- secretiveness
- aggressive or acting out behaviour
- prostitution
- involvement in child pornography
- inappropriate understanding of sexual behaviour and practices

- poor peer relationships or changed relationships
- compliance
- frozen awareness
- use of drugs
- restlessness.

The child sexual abuse accommodation syndrome

In 1983 Dr Roland Summit developed the model of the child sexual abuse accommodation syndrome (Summit 1983). This is a simple and logical model which gives understanding of how the child reacts to the sexual abuse. The syndrome has five stages. These are described separately here in terms of the behaviour of the adult and the child, as this gives practitioners insight into how the behaviour of the perpetrator informs the child's accommodation syndrome.

Stage 1 – Secrecy

- The adult either covertly or overtly convinces the child that the sexual abuse is a secret. Overtly this may be reinforced by the use of verbal threats. Covertly this may be by the use of body language, signs and signals. The adult uses the child's isolation and takes advantage of the child's helplessness.

- The child's concept that the adult is powerful and they are helpless reinforces the secrecy aspect. The child is likely to be confused, fearful or ambivalent. They may enjoy the attention which they receive or be afraid that bad things will happen if they disclose the abuse.

Stage 2 – Helplessness

- The adult uses the 'natural' power they have over children, and this produces a relationship where power and control determine the interactions. This is reinforced by comments such as *no one will believe you* or *no one cares about what happens to you.*

- The child is placed in a position of feeling powerless to stop the abuse. Eventually they stop trying to protect themselves physically: they go physically limp, withdraw or 'dissociate'. Dissociation is one way in which children are able to survive the sexual abuse by 'escaping' mentally while the abuse is happening. Children do this in different ways, but imagining they are outside of the body which is being abused is the method frequently used by children.

Stage 3 – Entrapment and accommodation

- The adult lies about or distorts his or her actions towards the child, for example telling them this is what all fathers do. This behaviour is repeatedly used.

- Children who keep their abuse secret become locked into a process of helplessness and entrapment. The child may eventually begin to blame themselves for what is happening, believing they are responsible for provoking the abuse. In the case of children who are physically abused, they see the abuse as a consequence of their bad behaviour. Emotionally abused and neglected children imagine they have unacceptable traits or behaviour. Abused children may also employ defence mechanisms (blocking) in an attempt to accommodate the abuse. In later life 'blocking' is used to prevent the abuse compromising the person's emotional health.

Stage 4 – Disclosure (delayed, conflicting and unconvincing)

- The adult may deny abusing the child if a disclosure is made, accusing the child of lying. This may be followed by attempts to reinforce the child's silence, either by personal intervention or by using other members of the family.

- Many children never disclose the sexual abuse they have suffered. In some cases disclosures may be accidental, some expressed in an angry outburst or may result from education/awareness (e.g. that fathers do not do this to their children). As Dr Summit put it, 'Unless specifically trained and sensitised, average adults…cannot believe that a normal, truthful child would tolerate incest [intra-familial abuse] without immediately reporting [the incident].' He sees this as the crux of the accommodation syndrome.

During this disclosure phase the child may test the reaction of others, for example the non-abusing parent, friends or teachers. Their reaction often informs the subsequent behaviour of the child. Rejection or refusal to believe by the non-abusing parent can reinforce the child's refusal to disclose and exacerbate existing feelings of powerlessness, confusion and guilt. A sympathetic or supportive response may promote full disclosure.

The emotional state of the child at the point of disclosure may lead to inconsistent accounts of the abuse being provided.

Stage 5 – Recantation/retraction

- The adult may continue to deny the abusive behaviour and may attract convincing support for his or her denial from family, friends and the child's siblings. The adult perpetrator or other adults may place the child under increasing pressure, accusing the child, for example, of 'destroying' the family.

- Many children maintain their disclosures and do not change their account of the abuse. However, some do and this is in part due to:

  o a feeling that they are not believed

  o the fear of being removed from home (e.g. to foster placement)

  o invasive medical examinations (in the child's mind a continuation of the abuse)

  o interviews with and fear of professionals.

Despite their experiences most children want to remain within their family and frequently want to stay with their abusive parent.

1.2 SALLY'S STORY

Sally is now 34 years of age. She lives in a bedsit with her current partner, John. They are both heroin addicts and John is HIV positive. Sally has refused to be tested; she does not want to know, and says that she does not care anyway. She has a lengthy criminal record, mainly for prostitution and shoplifting, and is currently awaiting sentence for offences of receiving stolen property. She says she needs to steal to fund her heroin habit. She has recently stopped prostituting herself because she was reminded of the sexual abuse she suffered in childhood, but she says, 'At least they have to pay for it – now I'm not the victim, they are'.

Sally has had three children, all of whom were removed from her care and have now been adopted. Her first child, Casey, was born when she was 15 years old and still in care. She had planned the pregnancy: 'I wanted something to love me'. She had a brief period looking after Casey in a residential family centre which specialised in assessing teenage mothers but this was terminated when Sally disclosed that she was having thoughts of harming her daughter. She said to her assessors, 'She was taking over my life like they had'.

Her two other children, Kylie and Jason, were removed from her at birth. By this time she was addicted to heroin and her lifestyle and living arrangements were deemed by the court to be unsuitable. Sally agreed for them to be adopted so that 'they would be protected from what happened to me'. She receives letters and photographs through the local authority 'indirect letter box contact' system, but tears them up without reading. 'I make believe they live in a big house with lots of toys and love and attention. I don't open the letters because I dread that one day it will say that they have been abused like I was. I don't want to look at the photographs because I would know by their faces if it was happening to them, even if they had not told anybody.' Sally refused to co-operate with the life story book for her children, fearing they would find out that she had been a bad mother.

Over the years Sally has self-harmed, cutting her wrists and legs. She says it releases the anger which builds up inside her; she says that she feels better afterwards. She has been admitted to psychiatric hospital on many occasions, as a voluntary patient and under compulsory order. She is on anti-depressant medication and that combined with the heroin helps her to forget what happened to her. She says that she uses heroin because at least it is her choice to abuse her body; it is something over which she has control.

She has made several serious attempts at taking her life and says that one day she will succeed, 'when the pain is more than I can bear any more'.

Sally was six years old when the abuse first started. She was then living with her mother, stepfather and three stepchildren in the centre of a large city. Her mother had an alcohol abuse problem and even before she began attending school she was helping to change nappies, feed and babysit. At first when her mother and stepfather came home from a 'night out', her stepfather would 'play fight' with her. 'Let's have some rough and tumble,' he would say. Sally would feel more physically hurt than anything. She recalled that he used to touch her intimately during these fun fights but she did not understand the significance of this until later. This play fighting led by stages to hugs and cuddles about which Sally felt uncomfortable. When she refused to give him a goodnight kiss, he would grab her and this was usually painful. When she offered her cheek he would grab her roughly and kiss her fully on the lips. Usually her mother would be out of the room when this occurred or was too drunk to realise what was happening.

She remembered the first time she knew that something was wrong. Her mother was in hospital following an assault by her husband which was officially recorded as a fall. She had suffered a concussion and a broken nose after he had hit her and pushed her down the stairs during an argument which Sally had witnessed. It was the day before her seventh birthday. He had been unusually pleasant towards her all day. After Sally had put her two younger siblings to bed he invited her to sit next to him on the settee. He was drinking strong cider and offered her some. She did not like the taste but he insisted she drink more. He then proceeded to digitally penetrate her vagina whilst he masturbated himself. The next day he bought her an expensive cycle. 'I could not even ride it,' she said, 'I was so sore.'

This was repeated several times more. Even after her mother's discharge from hospital she was usually too drunk to realise what was happening. Eventually the abuse became persistent and ended up in full penile penetration.

When she was 11, her stepfather started to bring home some friends. They would drink late into the evening and after her mother had fallen asleep they would take it in turns to abuse her. She said, 'By the time I was twelve I knew every sex perversion there was to know, he used to sit there and laugh whilst I was screaming for them to stop. Eventually I just cried inside, but no one heard me.'

When she was 13 she told her mother. Sally was sure she already knew but her partner's friends would bring lots of alcohol when they came and she began to realise that her mother thought more of the drink than her daughter. When she eventually told a teacher at school her mother beat her for 'spoiling everything. She called me a slag and a slut, she said I was the one who made them do these things to me. She said she never wanted to see me again – she never did – she died last year because of the drink.'

Sally went into care but found it impossible to settle. She withdrew her allegation in the hope her mother would forgive her. She moved from placement to placement. She did not like being in foster care; it was too personal for her. She preferred the anonymity of a children's home where she could avoid the close attention of adults. The self-harming, which started as superficial scratches to the wrists at 11 years of age, progressed to serious self-harming. She then marked other parts of her body. 'I just wanted to make myself ugly so no one would want to abuse me.'

When she was 18 years of age, Sally was able to disclose the abuse to her community psychiatric nurse, with whom she had developed a good relationship. They discussed going to the police but Sally was still afraid of her stepfather and what he might do to her and her half siblings. 'He always said he would kill them if I told anybody and it would be my fault not his. Perhaps I should have told somebody in case he did it to them after me, I don't know, I still feel bad in case he did.'

Sally believes that eventually she will commit suicide.

CHAPTER 2

The Abusing Adult

2.1 ADULTS WHO SEXUALLY ABUSE CHILDREN

The majority of adults who sexually abuse children are male; although there are some female abusers the numbers are very small.

Men who sexually abuse children

The behaviour which informs male sexual abuse is sex, power, domination and aggression. Males have a drive for sexuality often disregarding a close relationship with the partner involved. In contrast to women, men desire more sexual partners, are more aroused by visual cues and are more likely to use coercion to obtain their sexual partner (Buss and Schmitt 1993; Symons 1979).

Beckett *et al.* (1994) in a report of men in treatment found:

> typically emotionally isolated individuals, lacking in self confidence, under assertive, poor at appreciating the perspective of others and ill equipped to deal with emotional distress. They characteristically denied or minimised the full extent of their sexual offending and problems. A significant proportion were found to have little empathy for their victim; strong emotional attachment to children and a range of distorted attitudes and beliefs, where they portrayed children as able to consent to and not be harmed by sexual contact with adults... The men with the most problems in the above areas tended to be the most serious offenders.

Women who sexually abuse children

Women are generally more interested in emotional closeness and sexual contact within that relationship.

Allen (1991) reports that, when compared to male offenders, women who sexually abuse children are more likely to come from dysfunctional and abusive backgrounds. Physical, emotional and sexual abuse are often part of their experience (Faller 1988; Wolfe 1985; McCarty 1986).

Freel (1992) comments:

> they are more likely to have been sexually abused as children, that they have had a traumatic childhood; that they are more likely to co-offend with men; and they are more likely to use alcohol or drugs... There is [also] evidence that female abusers are more likely to be the mothers or close relatives of the children.

Matthews, Matthews and Speltz (1989) found three distinct categories of women abusers in their research:

- *Teachers/lovers* who are usually involved with adolescent or pre-adolescent boys. They want to teach them about sex.

- *Male-coerced offenders*, who initially abuse in conjunction with a male but may later abuse independently. This type of abuser is extremely dependent and non-assertive. This is most frequently seen in child protection cases. It is sometimes the mechanism through which the silence of the other adult is achieved or the exercise of power and control by the 'main' abuser is reinforced.

- *Predisposed offenders* who have been sexually abused from a very young age. They initiate the abuse themselves and usually abuse their own children. Their intention appears to be non-threatening emotional intimacy.

In my work with families where sexual abuse has been occurring I have encountered women who have been involved in the grooming process and in a small number of cases have included themselves in the sexual abuse initially. This is usually where, in an attempt to keep the male partner within their relationship, the woman promotes and permits the sexual abuse.

Adults with a learning disability who sexually abuse children

The sexual abuse of children by adults with a learning disability may be informed by the same issues as with adults who are within the 'normal' range of intelligence but there may also be other factors which inform the behaviour. These could include:

- The adult may have no other sexual opportunities. Where sexual relationships with other adults have been problematic in the past adults with a learning disability are likely to have a greater problem addressing and resolving this.

- Adults with a learning disability are generally less inhibited in their behaviour and this includes sexual disinhibition.

- This group of adults generally have poor impulse controls. Incidents of child sexual abuse by adults with a learning disability are most usually more opportunistic and less planned. They are not usually associated with grooming or the 'cycle of sexual abuse' (Wolfe 1985).

- Adults with a learning disability often feel more comfortable in the company of children where their intellectual performance is more compatible. Familiarity and friendship may be misunderstood by the adult. It is very likely that the child victim will be known to the adult.

- Adults with a learning disability often experience poor attachments and prior sexual abuse. Children with a learning disability are often seen as more vulnerable by adults who target children for sexual abuse. Therapeutic input may not be as successful in helping such children to deal with their abusive experiences and they therefore remain unresolved in adult life.

Internet offending – accessing child pornography

There is no one type of Internet child pornography user and not all such adults are involved in 'hands on' sexual abuse. Equally adults who sexually abuse children may not access child pornography on the Internet.

Cooper, Murphy and Haynes (1999) in studying the psychological typology identified the following categories of Internet child pornography users:

- *Recreational users* access child pornography sites on impulse or curiosity, or for short-term entertainment. They are not necessarily seen to have issues associated with child pornography.

- *At-risk users* are seen as vulnerable adults who have developed a specific interest in child pornography. They may not have been sufficiently determined to do so if it had not been for the relatively easy access of the Internet.

- *Sexual compulsives* have a specific interest in children as sexual objects and seek out child pornography.

Krone (2004) in identifying offending typology suggested the following groups:

- *Browsers* may come across child pornography accidentally but then save the images. They do not network with other offenders and make no attempts to avoid detection within their computer. Their browsing is an indirect abuse of children.

- *Private fantasisers* are offenders who create digital images for personal use to satisfy their own sexual desires. They do not network, do not have secure computer systems and their browsing is an indirect abuse of children.

- *Trawlers* seek child pornography on the Internet through open browsers. They may network minimally, do not have secure computer systems and their browsing is indirect abuse of children.

- *Non-secure collectors* seek child pornography in non-secure chat rooms and other open levels of the Internet. They have high levels of networking and do not employ secure computer systems. It is an indirect abuse of children.

- *Secure collectors* are members of a paedophile ring and have sophisticated methods to secure their computers. It is an indirect abuse of children. Given the hidden levels of the Internet they occupy they have access to a wide range of images. Collection may become obsessive as could careful cataloguing and cross-referencing. The collection may become an end in itself.

- *Groomers* develop online relationships with children and send pornography to children as part of the grooming process. Grooming is an indirect abuse but it is intended to lead to the sexual abuse of the child. They may or may not be involved in networking with others.

- *Physical abusers* (sexual abusers) for whom the interest in Internet child pornography is part of their paedophilic behaviour. Some record their abuse on computers. They may or may not network.

- *Producers* record the sexual abuse of children for circulation to others. They may also be distributors.

- *Distributors* circulate child pornography on the Internet. In some cases their interest is purely financial. Adults who access Internet child pornography and share images are distributors to some extent or other and whether or not they are involved in direct or indirect abuse of children is dependent on any other category to which they may belong.

The assessment framework

This assessment framework uses the same principles and checklists irrespective of the gender of the abusing adult. However, in the case of adults with a learning disability, although the assessment material will usually be the same, the style of the assessment sessions must be performed by practitioners who are experienced at working with this client group. Given that the majority of abusing adults are male and the partner female, the case study is framed in those terms.

The model of child sexual abuse

Finklehor (1986) produced a four-factor model for 'child molesting':

- *Emotional congruence*: Children are seen by the adult to be attractive because of their low level of dominance and the adult's socialisation to dominance, if the offender is immature, has low self-esteem or is aggressive. (Practitioners should seek to identify whether the adult's alternate sources of sexual gratification may have been blocked or prevented in some way.)

- *Sexual arousal*: Children may be seen to be sexually arousing because of the adult's own experiences, for example being the subject of sexual abuse or experience as a child. Sexual trauma and/or experience may remain as a conditioned response and create sexual attraction to children. Alternatively, child pornography may be a vehicle for sexual interest and arousal.

- *Blockage*: Some adults have difficulty forming relationships with other adults. This may be related to sexual anxiety, poor heterosexual skills or attitudes towards sex.

- *Disinhibition*: This occurs when the adult overcomes inhibitors through the use of drugs, alcohol, cognitive distortions or where levels of stress are created because of situations/circumstances and the adult's inhibitors are disrupted. Research has found that sex offenders are most likely to engage in deviant sexual fantasies following stressful events (McKibben, Proulx and Lusignan 1994 as cited in Marshall 2006).

Finklehor (1986) also identifies four pre-conditions to the sexual abuse of children:

- The adult must be motivated to offend.

- He or she must overcome internal inhibitors (e.g. by telling himself or herself it is just a bit of fun).

- He or she must overcome external inhibitors/external obstacles (e.g. by finding privacy).

- He or she must overcome the victim's resistance (e.g. by befriending/establishing trust).

Offenders are typically classified by their motivation to abuse. Groth *et al.* (1982 as cited in Bagley and King 1990) classified offenders as either 'regressed' or 'fixated'.

Regressed

- The sexual attraction to minors is not manifested until adulthood.

- Their sexual conduct until adulthood is similar to their peer group.

- Their interest in children is either not cognitively realised until adulthood or it was recognised early on and repressed because of the social taboos with which it is associated.

Fixated

- Fixated offenders are most often adults who are maladaptive to social norms.

- This offender 'identifies' with children and may see himself like a child.

- Such perpetrators sometimes resort to collecting articles belonging to the child as an outlet of their repressed desires.

- The abuse is often pre-conceived and rehearsed, and is not typically alcohol or drug influenced.

The adult's motivation to sexually abuse children

Each adult who sexually abuses children has a specific set of factors which motivate him or her and it is most helpful if this is understood both in terms of evaluating the risk that he or she poses to children and for the development of a child protection plan.

Motivation

There are a number of features which motivate adults to sexually abuse children and the following list incorporates the main motivators:

- *Jealousy.* This can come from within the adult relationship and may also be connected to a need for revenge.

- *Anger.* This can be generated from the adult's own experiences in childhood, including being the victim of sexual abuse themselves, a personality disposition inclined to anger or the circumstances in which the adult finds themselves. The anger is projected rather than contained.

- *Intra-familial abuse.* This occurs when a 'loving' relationship which comes from conventional family attachments becomes distorted by the adult and becomes one which includes sexual abuse.

- *Anger and conflict within the family.* An initial resentment occurs between the adult and the child because the child perceives the adult as someone who is taking away their mother or father. Alternatively, the adult resents the child's relationship with the mother or father. In the case of new partners or step-parents the adult may feel they are not accepted.

    The adult attempts to exercise some power in order to control matters and the child becomes resistant and defiant. Unrealistic expectations or impositions are had of the child and the adult becomes inconsistent and angry. The adult becomes increasingly frustrated by his or her impotence to deal with matters and may begin to see the child as being always wrong and never right.

    The age of the child is not a determining factor. A power struggle develops or the child withdraws and gives in to the adult. The adult feels the need to reinforce their control or neutralise the threat the child is perceived to be. This child should not be seen to be responsible for provoking the abusive response from the adult as a result of this behaviour. There are families where the adult's sexual abuse of the child will be seen by them as a way of gaining retribution on the partner.

    In some cases the adult's response is to become physically abusive and this may be informed by a need to punish, control and humiliate the child. In other cases sexual abuse occurs and issues of control and humiliation are more likely to be seen.

- *Sexual gratification*: This motivation for the sexual abuse of children should in no way be underestimated. It informs the behaviour of the adult and the need for sexual pleasure can be either spontaneous or well rehearsed and planned.

- *Power and control*: This particular motivation is usually seen as part of behaviour which dominates and controls individuals and families. Adults who are so motivated are likely to show signs of control in other aspects of behaviour. The sexual abuse of children is the ultimate way of demonstrating their power over the child.

The cycle of abuse

Each adult who sexually abuses children has a cycle of behaviour which should, if possible, be understood both in terms of evaluating the risk that he or she poses to children and for the development of a child protection plan.

Fantasy

Once the motivation to sexually abuse the child is engaged, the adult's tendency towards the abuse is often rehearsed through the fantasy stage. Fantasising about the sexual abuse or rape of children as part of masturbation confirms the interest in the child and reinforces the tendency to progress. Not all adults who fantasise about the sexual abuse of children will become abusers, but the predisposition to do so is clearly there. Adults who are motivated by anger are more likely to deny persistent fantasy but elevated fantasy at times when the cycle is active may be evident, for example, if the child is rejecting the adult's membership of the household or undermining the relationship between the adults.

Distorted thinking

In order to proceed from the process of thinking to the act of doing, the adult will distort his or her thinking to legitimise the abuse. Sometimes this pre-abuse thinking enables the adult to believe that they are doing no harm to the child. Sometimes the distortion enables the adult to see the child not as a person but as an object. In other distortions the adult convinces himself/herself that it is the extremity of their 'love' for the child which demands the sexual expression of that love. 'I loved her too much' is a distorted comment often heard. The distortion of thinking enables the adult to proceed in the false belief that they are causing the child no harm. It also allows them to overcome any resistance the child may offer.

Beliefs

In the case of some adults the extent of their distortion is such that they challenge the current laws and protocols in respect of children. For example, they argue that the age of consent is too high, or that children are more mature and sexually active now than when the laws were put in place. Some suggest that children, even very small children, enjoy the sexual activity and that it is society that is wrong rather than them. I have experience of one adult whose sexual abuse of children had been recorded over 20 years and who insisted that it was the professional intervention that caused the emotional harm, including self-harm, rather than the impact of his sexual relationship with the children.

Overcoming internal inhibitors

In order to progress towards the sexual abuse of the child the adult must first of all overcome his or her own internal inhibitors, that is, those concepts and belief systems which would prevent the conversion of interest to action.

There are likely to be adults who have an interest in children sexually but through an ability to control their desires, they do not progress to the sexual abuse of children. However, even with high or good internal inhibitors, sexual abuse could still be a possibility. It is the case that the better the internal inhibitors/controls, the more intense, persistent or strong would need to be the level of arousal and desire, before the sexual abuse of a specific child or children is actively sought.

There are a number of reasons why internal inhibitors are overcome and these can include:

- *Peer pressure:* This will involve friendships or regular interactions with adults who have an interest in children sexually. Their behaviour and belief systems can influence the adult. Observation and peripheral inclusion can become involvement. Group participation can have the effect of diluting individual feelings of guilt.

- *Fantasy:* Imagination can become a powerful disinhibitor, especially when it is associated with masturbation and orgasm. Heightened physical pleasure reinforces the behaviour and makes the move to action more compelling.

- *Child pornography:* This is an increasing area in which information and images are available to adults who may not have had previous access to others with similar interests or access to material which supports their interest. Children may be seen to be enjoying the act of sex and this overcomes, for some adults, the view that sexual abuse is a painful and frightening experience for children. For those with a more sadistic tendency, material which compromises the physical health and wellbeing of children may act as a disinhibitor.

- *Alcohol and drugs:* Alcohol and drugs act as a disinhibitor to behaviour which under other circumstances adults may well not consider. Alcohol is sometimes used as an excuse for or in mitigation of abusive behaviour. It would however be very unusual for drugs or alcohol to be the single cause of the sexual abuse of children by adults and I have not come across any such cases.

- *Anger, jealousy, revenge:* These and other emotions can be a significant disinhibitor, particularly in family situations, and should not be underestimated. Understanding the dynamics which are operating within the family becomes an important part of the assessment. It can inform child protection systems and address the essential 'safe' parent issues.

Targeting

Adults who sexually abuse children usually have a pattern of targeting. Some will target a particular type of parent, single, vulnerable, isolated and to some extent socially incompetent. They want to establish a dependency relationship where their behaviour is less likely to be challenged and where they exercise a significant level of power and control over the family's living arrangements and decision-making processes.

Others will be more preoccupied with a particular gender or type of child and expect to abuse them away from the family group. It is important for practitioners to understand how the adult targets children or families and what preference criteria is used. Where a particular type of child is selected, an understanding of the precise description and behaviour should be obtained.

The availability and vulnerability of children and families may sometimes be the only features needed to be targeted.

It is known that adults pass on to each other information about vulnerable families. It is therefore not unusual for families where children have been sexually abused to be targeted by other potential abusers. This makes the task of safe care work with families who have been victims an important part of their overall child protection plan.

Initial contact

There are many ways in which adults initiate contact with children:

- *Contact outside of families*: Many adults who target outside of families will engage in employment or recreation activities which expose them to working with children. Others will become involved with groups such as Scouts and Guides. The essential ingredients are that the children are not being supervised by their parents or carers and that the adult has some responsibility for and power over them. Activities such as swimming and athletic clubs, where a level of touch and opportunity exist, are also attractive for the adults.

- *Contact within families*: Adults who target children within families frequently enter those through relationships with the parent. Stepfathers, new partners and family friendships are all mechanisms to become involved within the family and enable responsibility and close contact with the children. Friendships with older siblings may also be a vehicle used to gain access to families.

Overcoming external inhibitors

External inhibitors refers to the management of circumstances which would usually be put in place to protect the child. People who are normally responsible for protecting the child need to be neutralised in terms of their care and protection function. The adult needs to establish the correct circumstances to be able to sexually abuse the child without risk of being caught. In order to do this he or she must create an environment where suspicion does not exist and where trust by other adults prevails. Some adults will do this by creating a 'loving' relationship with the other adult responsible for the care of the child, which appears to be mutually satisfying and reciprocal, thereby dismissing the notion that he or she is interested in any other form of sexual contact. Others will establish a relationship of power and control within the adult relationship which prevents any resistance to behaviour and silences criticism and/or concern. This kind of 'demanded silence' may be reinforced by physical and emotional abuse, similar to the way in which a child's silence may be achieved.

Overcoming the child's resistance

The adult needs to establish an abusive relationship with the child which prevents the child from disclosing but enables the abuse to continue. It requires the adult to manage and manipulate the child even when there is no actual contact taking place. This is typically achieved in the following ways:

- *Grooming*: This is the process which establishes a trusting and emotionally connected relationship with the child, from which the sexual abuse can take place. It has some features similar to the adult relationship but with two adults the resulting sexual relationship is consensual. With children no such consent can of course be given. Some adults are sufficiently practised at grooming that they are able to get the child to think and believe in the same way as the adult. Others convince the child that they are the initiator of the abuse and guilt is shifted from the adult to the child. Convincing the child that he or she is the cause of the abuse not only secures the sexual aspect of the relationship but reinforces the 'silence' principle.

- *Conditioning*: In this part of the process the adult slowly familiarises the child with the inevitability of the sexual abuse so that the child gradually accepts what is happening and their resistance is neutralised. In some cases the adult is able to do this so successfully that the child initiates the first sexual contact.

- *Bribes, treats, rewards*: Some children respond positively to treats, sweets and presents. It enables the adult to engage with the child; it permits the child to feel positive about meeting and engaging with the adult. The child may not consciously connect the treat to the abuse or understand that it is connected. In the same way treats after abuse will not necessarily be seen by the child as buying silence. However, the promise of future treats may be understood to be dependent on the child's silence and future availability. Reinforcement can be achieved by making the child believe they have been 'paid' for the sexual abuse and are therefore as guilty as the adult.

- *Threats, punishment and fear.* The use of negative reinforcement as a means to ensure the silence and co-operation of the child is not unusual. Comments can include death threats against the child, other siblings or birth parents and are often reported by children finally disclosing abuse. Fear of prison, separation from family and family disintegration are other tools designed to retain silence and make the child available for abuse. (Reports from adult survivors of abuse talk about this aspect of the abuse they suffered as the most lasting and damaging. Adults remain emotionally compromised and suffer ongoing emotional ill health because of the fear with which they lived, in some cases throughout the majority of their childhood.)

- *Physical violence.* The act of sexual abuse is in itself an act of violence. Children are not able to tolerate invasive sexual abuse without suffering great pain. Some adults preserve their abusive relationships with threats of even more pain. Some adults include violence within the abusive process. The fear of more or persistent abuse creates the climate of fear the adult wants to establish in the mind of the child.

Re-targeting

Some adults will be targeting, grooming or looking for their next victim whilst they are sexually abusing the current child victim. Therefore practitioners should not assume that the child who has disclosed is the only one who has been abused or that no other child is being groomed to be the next victim. Whilst adults might deny interest in other children of the family, unless there are compelling reasons why a particular child has been selected for abuse it should be presumed that other children in the family have been targeted, are being abused or will be targeted for abuse in the future. Some adults will sexually abuse stepchildren but not their own birth children; others see all children, whether birth children or not, as potential victims.

Ending the abuse

There are many reasons why adults will cease the abuse of a particular child or children in general. There is no significant evidence that adults stop abusing children because they make a conscious choice to do so without any other intervening features. Adults stop the sexual abuse of children because:

- they have been caught

- the child has made a disclosure

- the safe parent has found out and is protecting the child

- the family has moved away

- the adult has moved away

- the child has confronted the adult and the balance of power has shifted to an extent that the adult feels disempowered to continue the abuse or the child empowered to prevent it continuing

- the adult has moved on to the abuse of another child

- the adult has passed on the child to another adult.

The abuse cycle

Wolfe (1985) produced a cycle of abuse which begins with the perpetrator having a poor self image. This produces an expectation of rejection which results in the person withdrawing and being unassertive. Sexual fantasies are used as compensation and lead to masturbation for sexual gratification.

The cycle then moves on to converting thoughts into action. Once the child is identified and targeted the perpetrator needs to groom the child for the abuse. This involves various techniques which enable the perpetrator to establish control over the victim, overcome resistance and create the circumstances in which the abuse can occur.

Once the abuse occurs the perpetrator has feelings of guilt which are to an extent diminished by the process of distorted thinking. Feelings of low self-esteem remain and the perpetrator is ready to repeat the cycle.

The cycle is not specific to all adults who sexually abuse children. It is an overall picture of the abusive process. Within that there will be differences because of the circumstances of the abuse. For example, abuse outside of the family may have a different cycle and different timescale from abuse which occurs within families.

Each adult will have their own cycle which is likely to be repeated. It is important to understand the construction of the individual's particular cycle and how that was implemented for a number of reasons:

- to understand the adult's unique cycle

- to understand how and when any safe parent systems were undermined

- to inform any individual treatment programme for the adult

- to develop appropriate child protection plans for the child or other children

- to assist with the child's individual therapy or support programme and for any 'keep safe' work which the child may need

- to assist with the assessment of the non-abusing adult.

Types of adult who sexually abuse children

Fixated paedophile

This adult may be interested in children of both genders or of only one. They are preoccupied with the abuse of children and it dominates much of their thinking and behaviour. It is felt that some adults who have such an interest manage not to convert their interest into action. Although they will claim that the sexual relationship is based upon love, that is discredited as the child will be rejected once they have gone beyond the preferred age the paedophile targets. Fixated paedophiles often have contact with each other and exchange information about children they have abused and families who may be vulnerable.

Whilst individual aspects of paedophilic behaviour may not cause concern the accumulation shows a determined character, motivated by the desire to sexually abuse children. Because paedophiles present as nice, normal people with good communication skills and often settled long-term employment, practitioners should not be misled.

Being caught does not mean that they will stop abusing children. They are more likely to move to another area and begin again. The behaviour is compulsive, the motivation significant.

Fixated paedophiles present with the following characteristics:

- The main interest is in children.

- Their behaviour is predictable and repeating.

- They do not generally have good relationships with other adults.

- A parenting approach is used with the children (a pseudo-parenting approach).

- They adopt a relationship approach which has a seductive element.

- They will have a specific pattern of behaviour which has been successful and is therefore repeated. It is important that this pattern is understood.

- The fixated paedophile will be patient when forming relationships with children and careful that the elements of secrecy and privacy are maintained.

- They will use child pornography and erotica.

- They will sometimes introduce the child to sexual matters by showing adult pornography in order to introduce sex as 'normal', and reduce the inhibitions and fears the child may have.

- Fixated paedophiles often have friends who are paedophiles and may only have such friends. Information will be shared between them about vulnerable children and families.

- They will have significant cognitive distortions which can be presented in a very convincing fashion.

- They will frequently deny the abuse or insist that the sexual abuse is a 'one off', completely out of character, and will never be repeated.

- They are more likely to live with parent(s) or by themselves. They do not usually have a partner.

- They may, however, be married but this will be to give the impression of adult heterosexual normality. (The relationship will need to be explored by practitioners to establish whether it is emotionally and sexually reciprocated.)

- They are more likely to be an older adult.

- There will be no pattern of relationships.

- They enjoy the company of children.

- They will target vulnerable families whose children they can exploit more easily. Families who have previously suffered physical abuse and emotional neglect will be targeted as being particularly vulnerable. They may engage with the parent to gain access to the children. Parents with some learning disability or childlike qualities are often targeted.

- They will often attempt to gain access through clubs, societies and groups dedicated to the care, entertainment and recreation of children.

- They are likely to have fixtures and fittings at home which children will find attractive.

- They will usually target children of a particular age, sometimes with particular features and sometimes specific aspects.

- They will describe children in terms of their innocence and purity.

- They will want to establish privacy with the child by offering to undertake primary care, often at some apparent inconvenience to themselves.

- An interest in sexually abusing children may begin in adolescence and this should be explored by practitioners.

- They show children that they are able to listen to what they have to say and have good and age appropriate communication skills for children.

- They make children feel special and provide them with a level of attention which they enjoy.

- They will present as a 'nice person', someone of whom other adults would not be suspicious.

- They will establish a position with parents characterised by trust and integrity.

- Status is important to the fixated paedophile. They will prefer to present with a level of authority, for example a 'leader' or 'organiser'.

Inadequate paedophile

The inadequate paedophile will have a level of impairment, for example suffer from mental ill health, learning disability or some intellectual impairment. The following characteristics are likely to be seen:

- They may be seen as inadequate because of intelligence, social isolation or mental illness.

- Sexual abuse may be motivated by interest/curiosity and with, for example adults with learning disability, may be age related. (If the adult has a mental age of eight years, children of that age may be targeted. The adult with learning disability would not appreciate the child would not have the same level of physical development or sexual urges.)

- They are likely to see children as non-threatening, and are likely to perceive them as peers.

- Relationships involving or including sexuality may be impossible to establish and maintain.

- Issues of frustration and anger are not managed well and will sometimes remain unresolved.

Intra-familial abuser

This type of sexual abuse occurs when the adult is sexually attracted to his or her birth children and/or stepchildren. It is based upon the family unit and is therefore the one more likely to be encountered by practitioners working in the field of child protection.

Adults may be sexually attracted to their children or stepchildren but successfully manage those feelings and set appropriate boundaries within the family. Adults with abusive tendencies will establish relationships with the parent in order to gain access to the children and their pattern is described in the section on paedophiles.

For those adults who begin to develop sexually abusive relationships with children of the family the process is often a gradual one. Once the adult is committed to sexually abusing the child he or she will develop cognitive distortions about the sexual relationship. In order to justify and normalise his or her behaviour, the adult will be in denial that the behaviour will in any way be bad for the child. The process of abusing the child is made more easy because:

- of the extent of contact the adult has with the child

- of the availability of the child

- of the availability of the child at times of undress/bathing/dressing

- of the presumed authority the adult has over the child

- the child is likely to have some feeling of being cared for and cared about by the adult

- trust is likely to have been created

- opportunities for nudity and intimate care are available and seen as a 'normal' part of family life

- hugs, cuddles and kisses are a 'natural' part of the adult/child relationship.

In the case of parents, step-parents and partners who sexually abuse children, these acceptable aspects of adult care develop into sexual gestures. For example, the kiss on the cheek becomes a kiss on the lips, becomes an adult kiss using the open mouth and tongue. The adult may manipulate the child's behaviour so that the child feels they are the initiator of these developments. Issues of guilt are created and the child becomes ensnared in the process.

Once engaged the child can remain a victim of the abuse for many years. There is often no escape for the child; the abuse continues until the child discloses and is believed, the adult relationship ends for other reasons or the child grows up and moves away. In some cases the child feels sufficiently empowered to challenge/resist the abusive behaviour. Sometimes the sexual abuse will be persistent, at other times periodic. Throughout, the child's physical and emotional health will be significantly compromised.

Detection is avoided and the silence of the child guaranteed by the use of threats and physical violence. These are sometimes directly to the child but at other times directed towards other members of the family, for example if the child refuses the adult's sexual advances the other adult is physically assaulted. The child is made to feel responsible for what has happened: 'See, it's all your fault, you made me angry.'

Frequently the adult will be less overt. Manipulation and subtle threats are used, for example that the child will be taken into care or the family will be split up.

Fathers and stepfathers may use the following cycle of sexual abuse:

- Play fighting, tickling and tactile engagement can be used.

- Aspects of intimate care are undertaken, for example bathing. The adult may 'accidentally' allow a level of nudity, sometimes walking into the bathroom when the child is bathing, at other times walking in on the child in a state of undress.

- The adult experiences sexual arousal.

- Fantasies become part of the adult behaviour.

- The adult may use sex education to introduce the child to sexual knowledge and 'interest'.

- Play fighting becomes more intimate, tickling touches intimate parts of the child's body.

- Sexual contact is made; this can include the adult using the child's body or vice versa.

- The 'silence' principle is engaged, either through threats, coercion or bribes.

- The adult's cognitive distortions are engaged, for example that the child is not being harmed by the abuse and/or enjoys the experience.

- The sexual abuse is now established and its pattern and frequency is established. The adult now finds it difficult to stop the sexual contact and it is usually some outside intervention which brings the abuse to an end.

Anger-motivated intra-familial abuse

The cycle of this type of sexual abuse is described above; it is the motivation which is different.

In some cases a level of family dysfunction or perceived dysfunction has created the climate for this kind of abuse to occur, but that should never be considered to be the trigger for the abuse. There will be a dynamic within the adult which inclines towards the abuse of children.

In the case of adults joining the family the issue of access to the children for the purpose of abuse must be considered.

The adult motivated by anger is more likely to remain within the family and more determined to do so.

The adult may be seen in the following terms:

- He or she is seen as an asset to the community, often helping less fortunate people.

- He or she has a good work record and is seen as conscientious.

- He or she is seen to be 'in charge' within the family home and controlling of family matters.

- He or she makes the decisions for the family.

- The abuse almost always occurs within the home.

- The abuse is often described as 'out of character' and usually seen by others as being so.

- He or she believes they have the right to love and affection and are motivated by anger.

- He or she sees his partner and children as 'possessions'.

2.2 BEGINNING THE ASSESSMENT

The majority of child protection assessments are best and most appropriately conducted in the family home where the client and family feels most comfortable. In their own home they are more likely to be relaxed and feel more empowered by the process. It also allows the assessor some insight into family life, for example who visits or knocks on the door. During an assessment some years ago the issue of drug misuse and possible supply of drugs was an issue. The client denied using drugs and claimed never to have previously been responsible for the supply of drugs to others. During assessment sessions the door bell rang frequently. The client would leave the room and whispered conversations would take place at the door. One visitor blatantly walked into the house and announced he had come to 'buy some gear'.

However, there may be very good reasons why the abusing adult is not interviewed at the family home. They may have been required to leave as part of the court proceedings. The perceived risk to other children of the family may be too great. They may be living in circumstances which are not appropriate for the sessions. Issues of risk to the assessor may have to be considered. Confidentiality must be a consideration at all times. In the event that the family home is inappropriate an agreed venue should be sought. That can often be the office of the adult's solicitor where he or she is unlikely to feel disadvantaged.

In the absence of an agreement the assessor may need to exercise some management of the process. This should be done in an appropriately assertive rather than authoritarian fashion.

Some assessments of families are conducted by two professionals working together, others by single professionals. Where professionals are working together it is crucial that they understand each other's style of interviewing and exchange information constantly. Where two professionals are working together, each assessing one adult within a relationship, information exchange and collaboration is vital. The adults' relationship with each other may require a joint interview as may other sessions.

The principles of assessment

Before the assessment sessions are commenced, the practitioner should have access to any background and current information in respect of the adult. It is important to establish what is already known about the adult and that might include the following information:

- childhood and family background

- any previous child protection concerns within any category of neglect or abuse

- a detailed record of any criminal history

- details of any previous allegations of sexual abuse

- a list of previous charges of sexual offences, including offences for which the abusing adult was not convicted

- contact with any professionals previously and/or currently working with the adult which may be of interest or relevant to the proposed assessment.

Some of the information may be confirmed and other parts suspected or alleged and account should be taken of this in constructing the sessions.

The assessment sessions

The way in which the assessment sessions are arranged and constructed depends to some extent upon the circumstances of each case, the time constraints involved and the availability of resources. It is important however that practitioners plan the sessions and that preparation and review time is included.

It is recommended that a revisit of previous sessions is made prior to each visit and that after each session time is taken to make notes about the interview and to record impressions gained. Questions raised in the mind of the practitioner should be noted as they may inform subsequent sessions. All information gained during the sessions, thoughts, notes and review comments should be kept as a detailed record of the assessment. Where matters are before the court they are often required for evidential purposes and are an essential requirement of the Code of Guidance for Expert Witnesses in Family Proceedings (Department for Constitutional Affairs 2003).

The following areas of information would normally form the basis of each assessment of the abusing adult. Additional sessions may be needed to address specific issues or where further information is required:

- chronology

- experiences from childhood

- perception of self

- previous relationships

- current relationship

- perception of his or her children

- sexual history

- offence history

- account of sexual abuse of child(ren)

- response to previous treatment programmes

- future aspirations for self, family and abused child.

In respect of the non-abusing adult the following additional issues will need to be addressed:

- attitude to offence

- ability to protect.

Time should be spent during the first visit to develop a rapport with the adults being assessed. Periods of rapport may be needed prior to each session and 'time out' may be required if the adult is becoming agitated, defensive, angry or displaying any other emotional response which may compromise the information being collected.

Feedback should be given appropriate to the assessment although practitioners should remain as neutral as possible when giving feedback. An overly optimistic or pessimistic feedback could well contaminate future assessment sessions.

2.3 ASSESSMENT OF THE ABUSING ADULT

The assessment of the abusing adult must address the overall risk posed to a specific child and often in respect of a specific child and family group. In order to achieve this the following information should be collected and understanding gained. It is necessary to:

- understand the person's background and evaluate how that has informed his or her behaviour

- understand his or her current thinking, concepts and belief systems

- understand the motivation to sexually abuse the child

- understand the perpetrator's cycle of abuse

- understand the type of sexual abuse category the perpetrator falls into

- evaluate his or her offending behaviour, specifically the sexual offences, and identify the level of risk posed to children

- examine the person's desire and capacity to change

- explore the perpetrator's relationship with his or her partner, if relevant and appropriate, to establish whether or not safe care systems can be put in place

- identify possible interventions and services which may reduce the risk posed to the child and which may help reduce any risk posed by the perpetrator.

The assessment of adults who have sexually abused children is one where there is a real likelihood that tensions will exist and some angry emotions be expressed by the adult. A level of selective information, misinformation or avoidance to provide information is likely to be evident. It is important that these issues are confronted if that is necessary.

It is equally important that practitioners interviewing adults who have sexually abused children bear in mind the following.

Previous abusive behaviour

The adult may not have other recorded offences, but it is possible that he or she has sexually abused other children. Practitioners should presume that may be the case and indicate that to the adult. Some adults will then accept that and disclose other incidents of abuse. Even when the adult denies other incidents/offences it is helpful for the practitioner to bear the probability in mind during the assessment.

Offence claims

Adults may say that the behaviour is completely out of character, that they are usually a contributor to society. He or she will want to convince you of the good and charitable work they do. Comments are usually made about how he or she helps neighbours and the disadvantaged in the community. Some adults will say that the offence is the only time they have sexually abused a child. That is unlikely to be the case. Others will claim it was unrehearsed and spontaneous. The practitioner must look for the cycle used by the adult to challenge this comment.

Denial

Denial is frequently seen, sometimes as an initial denial which is subsequently retracted, at other times persisting throughout the assessment. Some adults believe they have done nothing wrong and can be very convincing. Others may deny recall, for example because they were drunk. The practitioner must always proceed on the basis that the adult has sexually abused a child and must reinforce that position whenever that is needed.

Behaviour justification

The adult may well justify their abusive behaviour with the following supportive comments:

'It's normal behaviour in some countries.'

'They should bring the age of consent down.'

'She was as willing as me, I did not have to force her.'

Projecting blame

This is another tactic used by adults. Victims are frequently blamed. Sometimes the adult may also blame their past: either it was neglectful or physically abusive. Some disclose that they were the victims of sexual abuse themselves. If adults were themselves abused as children this may give some understanding as to their perpetrator behaviour. However, many adults who were abused as children do not go on to abuse children themselves. It may be a reason why some adults go on to sexually abuse children but it must never be used as an excuse or justification.

Minimisation

Most adults who sexually abuse children will minimise their offending behaviour, the extent of the abuse and the effect they believe it had on the child. Like people who are reporting alcohol and drug misuse, an under report is to be expected.

Risk factors

As with all child protection work one of the best predictors of the future risk posed by the adult is his or her past behaviour. Claims that they will never repeat the behaviour and that they have learned the lesson should be treated with a healthy professional suspicion.

Distorted belief systems

Adults are likely to present with distorted thinking to justify their behaviour. Much of this thinking could well be reinforced by access to other adults and peer group pressure. Confronting those distortions is a vital part of the assessment process.

Consequences of being honest

Some adults will find it extremely difficult to be honest with the practitioner. Often there is much to be lost, for example the adult may have convinced his or her partner that they did not abuse the child. If an admission is made now, that may entirely compromise their relationship. In the same way if the adult's own family has believed the adult and then find out that he or she was abusing the child they may disconnect the family relationship. Being entirely honest may confront the adult with what he or she has done and that is something they want or need to avoid.

Comments made by adults who sexually abuse children

Dishonesty, distortion, justification and projection are all apparent in the comments made by adults who sexually abuse children. The partner or child are often blamed and the perpetrators often present themselves as the victims. The following comments have been made:

> 'If I didn't do it to her someone else would have.'

> 'Someone needed to break her in it might as well have been me, at least I did in a loving fashion.'

> 'I was drunk, I did not know what I was doing.'

'I woke up and she was there beside me, I thought I might have done something to her but I could not remember.'

'I was just loving her, showing how much I loved her.'

'I never hurt her, I was always gentle.'

'I am the victim in this, she seduced me.'

'I was tickling her and she moved my hand down below.'

'I was masturbating when she walked in on me, she just took over.'

'She had orgasms so she enjoyed it as much as I did.'

'She liked what I was doing to her, she never complained.'

'I was checking to see if she had an infection.'

'I was drying her after a bath and the towel slipped.'

'I was showing her what lads would do to her when she got older.'

Dynamics operating within the assessment

There are specific dynamics operating within any assessment and practitioners should be aware of those which specifically relate to the assessment of adults who sexually abuse children.

The conflict of motives

- The abusing adult will want to demonstrate that he or she has never been or is no longer a risk to children.

- Some adults will refuse to engage in the assessment process. They believe their lack of co-operation will frustrate the assessment or their previous history will compromise their position. Comments which confirm this might include:

    'You've already made your mind up.'

    'You won't give me a chance because of my past.'

- Some will give the impression of co-operation whilst being selective about the information provided and many even attempt to conceal significant information.

- Others will co-operate with the assessment sessions, describe in detail the abusive episodes and therefore attempt to persuade the practitioner that they are now a different person.

- Others will genuinely want to deal with their abusive behaviour and reduce the risk they present to children.

The level of available information

- This varies considerably from case to case. In some instances families or individuals may already be known to agencies. In others the disclosure by the child may be the first contact that professionals have.

- Where information is already available, this should be reviewed carefully. This is particularly important where adults may have been involved with other families. Information may be available about targeting behaviour, for example the kind of family selected by the adult. It is also very important to have all available information about previous offences.

- Whilst all types of offences help to build up a picture, offences of violence and previous offences of a sexual nature are of particular interest. These can be used for specific questions and to test the accuracy of the information provided by the adult during the free narrative part of the information collection. This will help to form a view as to the extent to which information is being withheld or selectively reported and assists with the final evaluation.

- Police reports of 'domestic violence' may also provide valuable background information and insight into the dynamics within the family.

- Video recordings of police and social worker interviews of children alleging sexual abuse (Department of Health 1992) also provide vital information and should be viewed if they remain available.

Dealing with denial

- As with other forms of child abuse, adults who sexually abuse children often deny their offence. Sometimes this takes the form of denial of extent. With physical abuse there can be a claim that injuries were over-chastisement rather than malicious assault. With emotional abuse a claim is sometimes made that the adult did not appreciate their behaviour was emotionally harmful. The same claim can be made in respect of neglect. In cases of child sexual abuse some adults may claim accidental abuse during aspects of intimate care.

- Some adults deny entirely the allegations made or convictions received. The denial has been seen in the following comments:

  'The whole thing is lies, she made it up because she is jealous.'

  'I was found not guilty.' (This is a reference to a finding in the Criminal Court where the standard of proof is 'beyond all reasonable doubt'. This is a very high standard of proof. In the Family Court the standard of proof is 'on the balance of probability'. This means that it is more probable than not that the adult sexually abused the child or children. Therefore an adult can be found not guilty in the Criminal Court but a 'finding of fact' can be made against him or her in the Family Court. The comment by the adult refers to the criminal matter but the judgement can still be made in the Family Court that he or she has sexually abused a child or children.)

  'I did not do it but I pleaded guilty so they could blame me and the child(ren) would not be taken into care.' (Because the other parent or adult did not sexually abuse the child(ren).)

  'They said that if I did not admit it the kids would be adopted.'

- Not all adults who are seen to present a risk to the sexual abuse of children have committed abusive acts against them. Some adults have pornographic photographs of children or store images downloaded from the Internet. Possessing such material is a criminal offence. Comments of denial include:

  'I was keeping them for a friend.'

  'They are not mine, someone must have put them there.'

  'It disgusts me but I was curious about it.'

  'Someone else must have put them on the computer before I bought it.'

  'They must have been downloaded after I sold it.'

Using material such as this might indicate the adult is in the initial phase or pre-abuse phase of behaviour. Alternatively the sexual abuse of children may be occurring concurrently to the viewing of child pornography.

It is fundamental and essential to the assessment that the abusing adult and non-abusing adult are made aware that the assessment is being conducted on the basis that the adult has sexually abused the child(ren).

The assessment may begin with the adult being in denial but as the work progresses, involvement and inclusion enable a move towards some level of acknowledgement. In some cases that process can be assisted by the practitioner using terms which enable the adult to feel more inclined to be less defensive. Comments which might enable this could include:

'She or he may have seen you and your partner having sex.'

'She or he might have thought that is what people who love each other do.'

'I bet you told him or her to go away sometimes but they did not.'

'I can imagine that when he or she touched your penis/vagina sometimes you told them to stop.'

'I should think there were times when you just wanted to give him or her a cuddle but he or she wanted it to go further.'

'I bet you thought he or she was already messing about with other men or women.'

'He or she would really like to be tickled.'

It is, however, important that the level of apparent collusion with the adult is thoughtfully managed and carefully planned. Adults who sexually abuse children are often very skilled at manipulation and can readily adopt and adapt what is said to serve their own purpose if and when the need arises. It is therefore very important that the practitioner subsequently revisits these comments and identifies them as part of the adult's abuse cycle cognitive distortions.

It is also important that the adult is able to see his or her role in the abuse, that of the proactive and actual abuser and not that of the passive and reactive victim in the episodes of abuse. Only if he or she is able to do this can it be concluded that change is possible or that therapeutic intervention is appropriate.

2.4 THE CASE STUDY

This case study is designed to illustrate the assessment of a male abusing adult and a female partner who is unable to protect her children from his sexually abusive behaviour. The checklists are answered in such a way that clear evidence is seen, for example, of unhelpful childhood and life experiences, distorted thinking and inappropriate concepts and belief systems. This is to assist practitioners in understanding the value of the systematic way in which the information is collected and the value of the checklists.

John is 42 years of age. He lived with his partner Rachel, 23, and their children, Stephanie, aged five and Jasmine, aged three. They have been together for seven years. Rachel has another daughter, Adel, who is nine years of age. Adel's father was the partner of Rachel's mother. He was sentenced to eight years in prison for the sexual abuse and rape of Rachel from the ages of 9 to 14 years.

When she was six years of age, Adel developed a persistent urinary infection for which her mother eventually took her to the doctor. Rachel told the doctor that Adel was also soiling herself and that she had become very withdrawn. Following a medical examination, Adel was referred to a community paediatrician who was of the opinion that Adel had been sexually abused. There was evidence of tears in her hymen which were consistent with digital penetration. Her anus had signs of possible abuse, being described as 'gaping'.

A subsequent medical examination of Stephanie and Jasmine revealed some irregularities in Stephanie's hymen and fingertip bruising on her inner thigh. She was interviewed by a police officer and social worker using the *Memorandum of Good Practice on Video Recorded Interviews with Child Witnesses for Criminal Proceedings* (Department of Health 1992) but made no disclosure of abuse. She became tearful and distressed to an extent that the interview was discontinued.

Adel was interviewed by a police officer and social worker, again using the Memorandum of Good Practice. Adel disclosed that John had been 'playing with her tuppence' usually when her mother was at the bingo, which she attended twice a week. She knew it was 'rude' but she was afraid to tell anyone because if she did he had threatened to hit her and lock her in the cellar where it was very dark and cold. He had hit her on several occasions when she had tried to resist him. Afterwards he would be angry with her; he would blame her for what had happened. She said she was very afraid when he was like this. According to Adel he would have his penis exposed and erect each time he abused her and from time to time he would ejaculate. She also disclosed that she was made to perform oral sex on him when they went out together in the car and he often ejaculated in her mouth. He had 'put it in my tuppence loads of times and up my bum. It really hurt but I was too scared to scream.'

John was not charged with the alleged abuse of Adel because it was felt that Adel would not make a reliable witness and because the experience of giving evidence would be too traumatic for her.

Care proceedings were commenced on the three children. Adel was made subject to an Interim Care Order and placed with local authority-approved foster carers. Her two half siblings were allowed to remain in the care of their mother under an Interim Supervision Order on the under-standing that John would live away from the family home. He went to live with a close friend of the family, Paul R, who is a Schedule 1 offender (Children and Young Person's Act 1933). However, following an incident when John was found to be in the family home in breach of the agreement reached, Stephanie and Jasmine were removed and are currently on Interim Care Orders. They are placed together but in a separate placement to Adel.

John has supervised contact with his children Stephanie and Jasmine twice per week, at a Family Centre. He does not have contact with Adel, who has said she does not want to see him.

Rachel has supervised contact with the children three times per week.

A 'Finding of Fact Hearing' has taken place and the judge has determined that Adel has been sexually abused by John on multiple occasions since the age of five. There was evidence from a consultant paediatrician to the effect that Adel's hymen was abnormal and indicated 'persistent abuse which was likely to have occurred over a significant period'. There was also evidence 'of a gaping anus which indicated penile penetration and which supported the disclosure made by Adel'. During the court hearing, John denied that he had intentionally abused Adel but she may have been 'accidentally touched' whilst he was bathing, dressing and undressing her as part of the family's daily routines. Immediately following the hearing he disclosed that he had probably sexually abused Adel on one occasion; he could not remember how old she was at the time. He reported that he had become sexually excited whilst bathing Adel and had slipped his finger into her vagina. He said that 'no harm had been done and she probably didn't even realise what had happened'. She had not complained and he assumed she had not found the experience unpleasant.

John would like to return to the family home and has asked for a risk assessment of him in respect of all three children.

Rachel wants to continue her relationship with John and wants to be assessed as a joint carer with him.

2.5 THE FAMILY STRUCTURE

The start point for all assessments is an understanding of the person's life. This will include their family, their chronology and their experiences in childhood and adult life. The behaviour of adults is a combination of the experiences they have had in their lives and the way in which those experiences are internalised or interpreted.

Some practitioners construct the family by way of a family tree whilst others complete the family structure by way of a free narrative report. Whichever way is chosen, practitioners should note the extent to which the adult feels connected to their family and the emotions which are generated from the descriptions and recollections.

There should always be an emphasis on the connection of the adult's life story with sexual experience and sexual abuse.

Checklist for family structure

1. What are the names of your parents?

2. Where do they currently live?

3. How often do you see them?

4. Describe your relationship with them.

5. Has there ever been any child protection concerns about them?

6. Have any allegations of sexual abuse ever been made against them?

7. Describe all your siblings, half siblings and step siblings as above.

Case study

John's family

John is 42 years of age.

John's mother is Jean P. She is 59 years of age and lives with her husband Robert P who is 63 years of age. John does not have a good relationship with his stepfather, who prevents John from having contact with his mother. They last had contact many years ago. John does not remember anyone being involved with the family other than the Education Welfare Officer because he did not go to school.

His father is John S senior. He is 69 years of age and his current whereabouts are unknown. John last saw him during a prison visit when he was about 12 years old. He has been told that his father was referred to locally as 'flasher' and that he was in prison on several occasions. He thinks that his father may have served sentences for sexual offences but does not know whether this involved children.

He has a half sister, Samantha, who is 38 years old (same birth mother). She lives locally with her two children, Reuben, eight and Rebecca, six. She does not have a partner. They do not have contact and John commented: 'She thinks every bloke is a pervert, she won't let blokes near her kids.' He does not know why this is the case.

Issues arising from this information

- John's relationship with his mother was not helpful to his childhood experiences.

- His father appears to have been a sex offender.

- He does not appear to have been close to his sister.

- Relationships in adult life are disconnected and he can not rely upon them as part of his support network.

2.6 CHRONOLOGY

As much self-report as possible should be used when collecting this information as this will indicate the accuracy of memory. It will also reveal the extent to which the adult is being selective about the information, is withholding information or is distorting the information. If prompting is needed this should be done only where there is felt to be no alternative.

Choices, even multiple choice options, for the adult should be avoided at this time.

If the adult refers to incidents of sexual abuse or child protection it may be helpful to explore it at this stage as the description could well be connected by them to that period in their life. If the adult does not mention any abusive episodes the specific checklist under 'experiences from childhood and in adult life' addresses the issue.

The information should not be challenged at this stage as it might make the adult more defensive and restrict the extent to which they feel able to co-operate. Allow the adult time to think and reflect. Anticipate difficulties and emotional distress as much as possible and allow 'time out' if that is needed. Be aware of the adult's body language as this may give clues to the extent of any emotional distress.

If prompting is needed use age focused questions such as age when siblings were born or when memorable incidents may have occurred. If the adult stops a helpful prompt may be 'What happened next?'

Checklist for chronology

1. Where were you born?

2. Tell me about your childhood.

3. Tell me about your adult life.

Case study

John's chronology

John was born in Newtown and brought up by his birth parents until he was three years old. He has no memory of his father being a member of the household. He has been told that he was in prison for some time during those three years.

When his parents separated, Robert P moved into the family home immediately. John said that as he grew up he was very angry that his mother had let Robert P into their home so quickly after the departure of his father.

John recalled being beaten regularly by his stepfather. He used to hide under the stairs when his stepfather was in a bad mood, which according to John was most of the time. When his mother tried to protect him she was beaten as well. They fled to refuges several times but, on promises from his stepfather, John's mother always went back to him. He always promised that things would change but they never did.

When John was five years old, his half sister Samantha was born. His stepfather became more and more abusive towards John and his mother. Samantha could do no wrong and was always given what she wanted.

In the kitchen there were two cupboards, one for John and his mother which usually contained corn flakes and tins of beans. The other was for Samantha and his stepfather and was always full of lots of different food and sweets. John had to sit at the table and watch them whilst he and his mother usually had beans on toast. He remembered once taking some sweets from his stepfather's cupboard. He was beaten so severely that he had to be kept off school for a week so no one could see the bruises.

When John was four years old he was befriended by a neighbour, Paul R, with whom John spent a lot of time. Paul R was subsequently arrested following a disclosure of sexual abuse by a nine-year-old girl. John was 13 years old at the time and initially disclosed to the police that he had also been sexually abused by Paul R but withdrew the allegation shortly afterwards. Paul R was subsequently convicted of the rape of the girl and the indecent assault of a 12-year-old boy and sent to prison.

When he was 15 years old John left home and for a while he lived on the streets. Eventually he went into a hostel and from there into a bedsit. When Paul R was released from prison John moved in to live with him.

From the age of 14 John was arrested on a number of occasions for criminal damage. At least two of these offences were committed against the home of his mother. Each time he was arrested he was so violent that he was also charged with assault on police officers. The offences are noted to have been committed by him alone.

When he was 17 years old, John was arrested and charged with the indecent assault of a boy aged six, but the matter was not proceeded with.

When he was 19 he was convicted of assault on a teenage girl and was given a two-year probation order and ordered to attend an 'anger management' course.

At 20 he was sentenced to three years in prison for a street robbery.

John met his first partner Mary when he was 23 years old and she was 16. They lived together at the home of Paul R for six years until Paul R was convicted of the sexual abuse of two female children who lived locally. He was sentenced to a term of imprisonment.

Mary left John when he was 34. According to John, Mary accused him of being violent towards her but he denied this. He said that he only hit her in self-defence when she was attacking him. (Information from the social worker and police indicated multiple referrals for domestic violence throughout their relationship, but Mary always withdrew her allegations and he has no convictions.)

John met Rachel the following year at a drop in centre. She was 15 at the time and pregnant. She moved into his house the day after they met. Rachel subsequently gave birth to Adel.

They have lived together since that time, obtaining their own accommodation three years ago. They have two children, Stephanie, five and Jasmine, three.

Three months ago, John moved out of the family home, following the allegations by Adel. He is currently living locally with friends. He initially refused to disclose details of these friends, but eventually said that there had been concerns about their behaviour with children and one of them had been convicted of offences of sexual abuse against children.

Issues arising from this information

- John's childhood was physically and emotionally abusive. He is likely to have experienced fear, anger and isolation.

- He was discriminated against by his stepfather.

- He witnessed his mother being physically abused.

- He learned nothing about being cared for, cared about and nurtured.

- His childhood was insecure.

- He was befriended by Paul R, a convicted sex offender, and describes their relationship in 'idealised' terms.

- His teenage years were characterised by angry feelings and expressions and subsequent involvement with the police.

- He showed signs of uninhibited aggression and a disregard for socially acceptable behaviour.

- There is evidence of his involvement in sexually offending behaviour.

- Allegations of violence are reported in his first relationship.

- He was 35 years old when he met Rachel and she was 15 years old.

2.7 EXPERIENCES FROM CHILDHOOD AND ADULT LIFE

When the chronology has been taken the practitioner should return to look at the adult's perception of their childhood in terms of their experiences and relationships. How emotional connections are made, issues of care perceived by the child and how the overall feelings of care and safety are felt are important. They inform the way in which the child is likely to behave in adult life.

If the adult was subject to any form of sexual abuse this should be explored at this stage in some detail as it is connected to childhood. There should be a separation from the child's experiences as a child and victim from the adult as an abuser or non-abusing carer of children who have been abused. The child as a victim will give insight into how he or she dealt with that aspect of their life.

The questions in this checklist are comprehensive and can be used selectively. Practitioners should be looking at aspects of the person's childhood which may relate to or inform issues of sexual abuse.

Checklist for experiences from childhood and in adult life

In respect of each adult with whom the child lived

1. Describe your father/mother.

2. Describe any other important adult with whom you lived or with whom you had contact during your childhood.

3. Say three things you liked about them.

4. Say three things you disliked about them.

5. Did they go out to work when you were a child? If so did they work shifts, did they work away from home?

6. How long did you live with them?

7. Did they have any particular difficulties when you were growing up (for example alcohol abuse)?

8. Were there ever concerns that they had sexually abused children?

9. What kind of things did you do together?

10. What would they do if you were naughty?

11. What did they consider was naughty enough to be punished?

12. How often did they punish you?

13. What was the worst punishment you ever received from them?

14. Were you ever punished when you felt you did not deserve it?

15. Did you get hugs and cuddles from them?

16. How often did you get hugs and cuddles?

17. Describe your relationship with them now.

Education

18. Describe your education.

19. Were you ever bullied?

20. What did you most like about school?

21. What did you least like about school?

22. Did you ever miss school? If so? how often and why?

About the relationship of the person's parents/primary carers

23. What kind of relationship do you think they had?

24. How well do you think they got on together?

25. Was either person in charge of the relationship? If so why do you think that was?

26. How often did they argue?

27. What kind of things did they argue about?

28. What happened when they argued?

29. Who came off best when they argued?

30. Were they ever violent to each other?

31. How did you feel when they argued or were violent?

32. Why do you think they behaved in the way they did?

33. Did they ever have arguments about sexual matters?

34. Did you ever see them have sex together or acting in a sexual manner with each other?

35. Do you think their sexual relationship was good, or bad?

36. Did either of your parents ever talk to you about their sexual relationship?

In respect of each sibling, step sibling or half sibling

37. How would you describe them?

38. What did you like most about them?

39. What did you like least about them?

40. Describe your relationship with them.

41. How much time did you spend together, playing or doing things?

42. What things did you do together?

43. What was the worst thing they ever did to you?

44. What was the worst thing you ever did to them?

45. What was the nicest thing they ever did to you/for you?

46. What was the nicest thing you ever did to them/for them?

47. How would you describe your relationship with them now?

48. Describe any ways in which you were treated differently by your parents.

49. Did any of your brothers and sisters ever do anything sexually inappropriate with you?

50. Did you ever witness them doing anything sexually inappropriate with each other?

51. Did you ever do anything sexually inappropriate with them? If so, what?

Perception of home

52. Describe your home as you were growing up. What was it like?

53. Who lived there?

54. Where did everyone sleep?

55. Describe the kind of meals you had.

56. Describe the kind of clothes you wore.

57. Would you say your family was poor or well off?

Perceptions of self in childhood

58. What kind of child do you think you were?

59. What was the happiest time in your childhood?

60. What was the unhappiest time in your childhood?

61. What was the naughtiest thing you ever did?

62. Describe something in your childhood which made you feel really proud.

63. Describe times in your childhood when someone really hurt you.

64. Describe things from your childhood which still upset you.

65. Tell me about anything or anyone who made you feel afraid.

Relationship with local community

66. What was the area like where you were brought up?

67. What kind of things did you do for play?

68. Who did you play with?

69. Describe any time when people picked on your family.

70. Tell me about times when members of the family were called names.

Overall perceptions

71. What kind of childhood do you think you had?

72. Describe three good things and three bad things from your childhood.

73. If you could have changed something about your childhood, what would it have been?

74. What do you think you have learned from your childhood about yourself?

75. In what ways do you think you take after either of your parents?

76. What do you think you learned from childhood about being a parent yourself?

77. What support does your family currently provide for you?

Adult life

78. Describe your life as an adult.

79. What work have you done?

80. What have you most enjoyed about your adult life?

81. What have you least liked about your adult life?

Checklist for adults who were sexually abused as children

1. How old were you when you were sexually abused?

2. Do you remember how you met the person?

3. How long did you know the person before you were sexually abused by them?

4. Describe what happened.

5. What things were you made to do?

6. How long did the sexual abuse last?

7. Did anyone else know?

8. Did you tell anybody? If not, why not?

9. Did you do anything to try to stop it? If not, why not?

10. Why did the abuse stop?

11. Do you remember how it made you feel at the time?

12. How do you feel about it now?

13. Have you ever had any help to deal with what happened to you?

14. If not, do you think you could be helped to deal with it?

15. Do you think any of your brothers and sisters were abused like you were?

16. Describe any subsequent incidents where you were sexually abused.

Case study

John's experiences from childhood and adult life

John has no purposeful memory of his father but made the following comments:

'He was a waste of space.'

'He was in and out of prison all the time.'

His mother worked occasionally as a cleaner when John was young. He made the following comments about her:

'She was a cow.'

'She never did anything when he was belting me.'

'She would lie – she used to tell people I had fallen or something when I had bruises.'

'She never paid me any attention.'

'She would hit me for nothing, mostly after he had belted her.'

'In her eyes I could never do anything right.'

'I loved my mum but she never loved me back.'

His stepfather repaired cars for people on the estate where they lived but John could not remember him having any other form of employment. John described him in the following terms:

'He was horrible.'

'He would beat me up for anything – he really enjoyed hitting me.'

'He was never kind to me, not even once.'

'In his eyes my sister could never do anything wrong, I could never do anything right.'

'He used my mam as a punch bag sometimes, especially if he had been drinking.'

'Why did he hate me when all I wanted was for him to love me?'

He does not recall being hugged and cuddled by either his mother or stepfather.

John felt his half sister was always favoured over him. He said their relationship was never close and made the following comments about her:

'She told lies to get me into trouble.'

'She used to love it when I was getting hit.'

'She would say I had hit her, even when I hadn't, so I would get belted.'

'I hated her, I still do.'

He said the relationship between his mother and stepfather was always violent. He used to lie in bed at night listening to them arguing and fighting.

He felt his life changed after he met Paul R. He made the following comments about him:

'It was the first kindness I had ever felt.'

'He used to buy me things, make me laugh, feed me proper food.'

'He was like the dad I never had.'

'I was devastated when he went to prison.'

'He had not done what those kids said he had – they were making it all up.'

'We are still mates, best friends, more like father and son really.'

'He knows I haven't done what they have said I have done to Adel.'

He described his happiest childhood experience as meeting Paul R and his saddest when Paul R was sent to prison. He was most frightened when his stepfather was hitting him.

He felt his childhood was all bad except for the time he spent with Paul R.

He remembers feeling angry all of the time when he was a child.

John said that he attended ordinary school but his attendance was poor in the last three years. He felt this was because he was unhappy at home. When asked to describe himself as a pupil he commented:

'I was a pain in the arse.'

'I nicked off a lot of school.'

'They said I was a bully. I suppose I was when I got older, but I was only getting my own back for what happened to me at infant and junior school.'

He has not worked for much of the time since he left school. He has been on Youth Training Schemes and worked on a casual basis for friends. He has not worked for the past seven years because of a problem with his back. He spends most of his time at home or visiting Paul R. He said he does not make friends easily and avoids other people most of the time.

He recalled the following three good things from his childhood:

1. time spent with Paul R

    2. stealing money out of his stepfather's wallet when he was drunk

    3. going on trips with school.

He recalled the following three bad things:

    1. being physically abused by his stepfather

    2. his mother not loving him

    3. when Paul R was sent to prison.

He learned the following lessons from his childhood:

Never to let people do him down.

To give as good as he got.

Never to let people abuse him.

When this was clarified John made it clear that he was referring to the physical abuse he suffered from his mother and stepfather.

John was asked what he felt about the conviction of his friend Paul R.

'He never did it, he was not like that.'

'He would cuddle me sometimes but he never touched me.'

'People said he was a pervert but he wasn't.'

'Sometimes I hated him when he paid attention to other kids.'

'I used to get really angry with him when he got friendly with other kids.'

'I wanted him to love me, and only me.'

I asked John if Paul R had ever acted in an inappropriate fashion with him.

'No, he never tried anything like that, never.'

'He wasn't a pervert, he isn't a pervert.'

Issues arising from this information

- This description is typical of children who did not feel any significant emotional connection to their adult carers and indicates an insecure attachment to those adults who looked after him during those important formative years.

- John's friendship with Paul R enabled him to feel cared for and cared about in a positive way. It is possible that he permitted a level of sexual contact with Paul R as a 'price worth paying' although there is no specific evidence to support that and professionals need to be careful how this is worded in any report presented to court or a decision-making setting.

- It is probable that he learned much about 'grooming' children and young people for abuse through his contact with Paul R.

- Child management systems were entirely negative. He was physically abused even in circumstances where he did not deserve punishment. He would learn nothing about positive parenting systems such as distraction, diversion, accommodation and compromise. Punishment and imposition would dominate his relationship with his adult carers.

- He would learn nothing about parental roles and responsibilities, the appropriate use of parental responsibility and parental authority.

- He would not gain any understanding of adult relationships which had elements of care and reciprocation. He would learn that problems are resolved with violence, that adult relationships are characterised by one being dominant and the other being submissive.

- His adult life features two relationships where dominant and abusive behaviour have been apparent.

- His relationship with Paul R has been ongoing throughout and the impact of this on his behaviour should in no way be underestimated.

- He either denies his offending behaviour or minimises it.

2.8 THE ADULT'S PERCEPTION OF SELF

In seeking to understand the adult, it is important for him or her to describe themselves without any help or prompting from the practitioner. This free narrative phase is important as it allows the adult latitude to include whatever they want in this description.

Where adults are initially unable to report themselves immediately some patience may be necessary. Practitioners should however be aware of the adult's desire to reflect themselves positively and should be alert as to whether or not rehearsal of response is occurring.

Some adults may genuinely find it difficult to describe themselves and some prompt may be required. If this is needed consideration should be given to neutral comments such as:

- Describe yourself physically.

- Describe how you are emotionally.

- How are you with other people?

Once this non-directive information has been collected the practitioner should begin to ask more precise questions. The checklist below is very detailed and practitioners may want to be selective about the questions they ask. Some issues may have already been dealt with in the free narrative phase.

In gaining an understanding of the person with a specific emphasis on the sexual abuse of children the adult's concept of themselves in respect of sexual issues should also be included. The questions in the second list may be appropriate. The checklist only looks at matters in a global manner and practitioners should be aware of the need to explore any answers where clues are given about sexual behaviour or experiences which are relevant to the sexual abuse of children.

Checklist for perception of self

1. Describe yourself.

2. Use words or sentences which you think describe you.

3. What do you consider to be the best thing about you?

4. What do you consider to be the worst thing about you?

5. What do you like most about yourself?

6. What do you like least about yourself?

7. Describe times when you like to spend time alone.

8. When you are alone what do you think about?

9. What kind of things make you happy?

10. When was the last time you were happy and why?

11. Describe the happiest you have ever been in your life.

12. How often do you feel happy?

13. What do you do when you are happy?

14. How long does your happiness last?

15. Are you a happier person now than when you were young? If not, why?

16. Are you a happier person in the last few years? If not, why?

17. What would be needed to make you happy?

18. What makes you angry?

19. When was the last time you were angry?

20. Describe the most angry you have ever been in your life and what happened.

21. How often do you feel angry?

22. How long does your anger last?

23. What do you feel like doing when you are angry?

24. What do you normally do when you are angry?

25. What do you do to try to control your anger?

26. How often does that work?

27. Would you like to be angry more often or less often?

28. How do you think you could achieve that?

29. Are you angry more often now than when you were younger? If so, why?

30. Are there specific people who make you angry?

31. Are there specific situations which make you angry?

32. What makes you feel sad?

33. When was the last time you were sad?

34. Describe the saddest time in your life.

35. What do you feel like doing when you are sad?

36. How often do you feel sad?

37. How long does your sadness last?

38. What do you normally do when you are sad?

39. Do you try to do anything to stop feeling sad?

40. How often does that work?

41. Would you like to be sad less often?

42. How do you think you could achieve that?

43. Are you sad more often now than when you were younger? If so, why?

44. Tell me about specific people who make you feel sad.

45. Tell me about specific situations which make you feel sad.

The worker can explore other emotions which are appropriate to the particular person, for example:

46. helplessness

47. despair

48. stress

49. despondency

50. feeling down

51. anxiety

52. any others.

Exploring the person's perception of their relationship / interaction with others

53. How would other people describe you?

54. How many close friends do you have?

55. How easily do you make friends?

56. Who is your closest friend?

57. Why do you think you are so close?

58. How do you get on?

59. What do your neighbours think of you?

Exploring the future

60. What would you like to be doing in one year?

61. What would you like to be doing in three/five/ten years?

62. What changes, if any, do you think you will make in the future?

Exploring overall perceptions

63. In your whole life, what percentage have you been happy, sad, in between?

64. At present, how much of the time are you happy, sad, in between?

65. Would you like to change that?

66. What would be needed to change that?

Checklist for perception of self – additional questions, specifically referring to perception of self sexually

1. Describe your sexual orientation.

2. When do you think you first had sexual thoughts?

3. How old were you when you started masturbating?

4. What did you fantasise about when you were masturbating?

5. Did you have any sexual experiences as a child?

6. Did your fantasies change as you got older?

7. How often do you masturbate now?

8. Describe all of the fantasies you have had in your adult life.

9. Have you ever fantasised about children when you have masturbated?

10. Have you ever fantasised about children when you have been having sex?

11. How many sexual partners have you had?

12. Do you think you are sexually attractive to the opposite sex?

13. Do you think you are sexually attractive to your own sex?

14. Do you consider yourself as being sexually unattractive to other people? If so, why?

15. What do you believe to be your most attractive sexual feature?

16. Do you feel confident about engaging in new relationships?

17. Do you like to get to know people before you have sex with them?

18. Have you ever been offered casual sex? If so, what did you do?

19. Have you ever paid for sex? If so, when, why and how often?

20. Do you consider yourself to be sexually active or not?

21. Would you like to have sex more often or less often?

22. Have you ever used pornographic material? If so, how often and do you still use it?

23. Have you ever seen any child pornography?

24. Have you ever downloaded any adult or child pornography from the Internet?

25. Do you know anyone who has downloaded pornography from the Internet?

Case study

John's perception of himself

John described himself in the following terms:

'I'm not a pervert.'

'I'm an ordinary guy.'

'I like children but I don't abuse them.'

'I can be noisy.'

'I am sometimes bossy at home.'

'I like things to be organised.'

'I do loads of things for people round here.'

'If I have something and somebody else needs it I will give it to them.'

'Everybody round here likes me.'

'Sometimes I shout but normally I am quiet.'

'I am a hard worker – work is important to me.'

'Sometimes I get down, when things like this crop up.'

'I'm committed to my family.'

He likes most about himself that he is generous and kind.

The thing he least likes is that people now believe him to be a pervert.

John does not like being alone and spends as little time as possible by himself. When he is by himself he keeps busy.

He is happy when things are organised and the children are doing as they are told. He enjoys spending time with Rachel although she gets on his nerves sometimes, as do the children. His happiest experiences involved spending time with Paul R when he was younger and when his children were born. When he is happy he tends to be noisy.

The present situation has made John very sad. Other things which make him sad include when things go wrong, when he thinks about parts of his childhood, particularly when he was with his mother and stepfather and when he sees children who have been neglected or abused. He feels sad when he sees starving children in Africa. He makes the children watch this so that they can appreciate how lucky they are. He would be happy if he could return to live with his partner and the children returned to live with them.

Lots of things make him angry. The removal of the children made him more angry than he has been for a long time and he lost his temper with Rachel, assaulting her and breaking her nose. Rachel initially agreed to press charges but subsequently withdrew her complaint. Sometimes the children would make him angry when they misbehaved and made too much noise. At times Rachel makes him angry when she does not do as she is told and when she does not support him with the discipline of Adel. He does not see himself as being any more angry than other people and less angry than most.

When he is angry he tends to shout and swear. In the past he has thrown things but the last time was just after he met Rachel and they were arguing because Adel was misbehaving. He said he has never assaulted Rachel previously. He has slapped her from time to time but only when she has been hysterical or has refused to do as she is told.

He does not have many friends but says the ones he has are important to him. His closest relationship is with Paul R who lives nearby and who John sees most days. He has been told by the social workers that Paul R should not have contact with children but John feels this is wrong because he does not present any risk to them.

He said his neighbours saw him as a 'good Samaritan' until the present situation. He is now insulted and verbally abused by them. Some of the local men have threatened to beat him up. He said, 'I feel like Paul R now – he has to stay in all the time because of the threats.'

He thinks that he suffers from stress from time to time and this can make him feel depressed and angry. He commented, 'Sometimes I think my head is going to burst.' He has been to the doctor because of stress and is on medication which he thinks has been prescribed for depression. At times he feels really low in mood and this can, at different times, make him feel angry, desperate and tearful. He has had thoughts of self-harming but has never done so: 'It's the prospect of causing myself pain that stops me.' Adel's behaviour, Rachel and life in general all cause him stress.

He perceives the early part of his life as being sad, the time with Paul R as happy and his adult life as being 'in between'. He was very happy after he met Rachel, except for the difficulties he had with Adel, but he has been very sad since he was arrested and had to move out of the family home.

John has never been seen by a psychiatrist. He was seen by a psychologist when he was 17 years old because of the allegations made against him by a six-year-old male child. He said, 'They tried to make out that I was a danger to kids because of what happened to me when I was little and that I needed some help but I refused because I hadn't done anything to that little boy.'

Sexual history

John described himself as heterosexual. He denied having any homosexual thoughts. During one discussion he said that he hated 'puffs' (homosexuals) but during another discussion he said that what people wanted to do sexually was their business.

John thought that most of the other boys about his age became sexually mature before him as they would all talk about it at school. He said that he tried to masturbate and could get an erection by thinking of the girls in his class at school but did not ejaculate for a long time. He tried to convince the other children at school that he was sexually mature and when challenged once he said that his ejaculation looked like treacle. He was the butt of jokes after that and this was a part of the bullying he suffered as he grew up. He once masturbated publicly to show his class mates that he could and did not know that a group of girls had been told and were looking on from a nearby hiding place. He said he was very angry about this for a long time. As he got older and stronger he sought out those who had taunted him and 'beat the crap out of them'.

John did not initially report the circumstances of his disclosure of sexual abuse by Paul R and when this was raised he denied that he had been abused in any way. In respect of the disclosure he said that he had been afraid when he was interviewed. He was told by the police that he must have been abused and agreed with them because they said he would be 'locked up' if he did not. When he had time to think about matters he retracted his disclosure. In respect of the girl who disclosed sexual abuse he commented:

'She was a tart, she and her mates were all the same.'

'They used to come round and ask him for money.'

'Paul would play fight with them.'

'Paul didn't do anything to them, not on purpose anyway.'

'Paul said they were taking money off loads of blokes for doing things with them.'

'They deserved everything they got.'

It was put to him that Paul R had a conviction for indecent assault against a boy at the time when he was spending a lot of time with John and that he had made an initial disclosure. Professionals would be suspicious that he might also have been sexually abused. John denied this. He was asked whether Paul R had ever been affectionate to him in any way and after some thought he said they used to cuddle up on the settee sometimes. John was asked if he ever shared a bed with Paul R and he admitted that he sometimes got scared in the night and went into Paul R's bedroom. He sometimes got into his bed and fell asleep. John was asked whether he had ever been touched inappropriately by Paul R, even if that was accidental, and he agreed that might have happened. When asked what accidental touches he remembered he said that sometimes when they were play fighting Paul R might grab his 'privates'. He agreed this was his penis. When asked how this made him feel he replied it was okay because 'no harm had been done'. I asked if he would have felt differently if the grabbing of his privates had been intentional. He thought for a while and shrugged his shoulders. When pressed for an answer he became angry and said, 'Look, no harm was done, he was just playing.' John denied any other sexual experiences during his childhood.

He said that he masturbated most when he was growing up. He reported that as he got older his fantasies 'got older'. He said he had never fantasised about having sex with children.

He has had three sexual partners:

- He said his first sexual experience was when he was 16 years old. He knew the girl from school and was aware that she was sexually active. He knew that she had taken money from other boys to have sex. They had met accidentally when she was walking home late one night; she had been drinking and was staggering. He followed her for a while and they 'got talking'. She said that men were useless, that she had never had good sex with any of them. He said he offered to put that right. They started to argue and 'she went mad, kicking out at me and shouting'. John said that he lost his temper and 'slapped her to get her to shut up'. He said they then had consensual sex. It was pointed out to him the girl might have felt under some duress to have sex with him but he denied that was the case. Asked if he thought the experience was pleasurable for her he commented, 'I don't know, I don't care, she got what she deserved.'

- His second sexual encounter was with his first partner, Mary. He said that Mary had a learning disability and was younger than him. They had known each other for about a week when they first had sex. He said they had sex a lot to begin with but then 'she went off the idea'. He liked sex at least once a day.

  He agreed they had tried different types of sex. He said he preferred to receive oral sex but Mary did not like that. There were times when he insisted and sometimes he would lose his temper when she refused. He agreed she would usually give in to his demands. There were times when they would begin to play fight and that would lead to them having sex. Once or twice he got carried away and this resulted in Mary receiving bruises.

- His third partner is Rachel. He described their sexual relationship as all right. He likes to have sex with her at least once a day although she is not as keen as he is. He believes that she has orgasms although he has never asked her. He feels certain that she enjoys having sex with him. He insisted that he and Rachel's sex life was so good that he would not want to have sex with anyone else. He still prefers to receive oral sex. When he was told that Rachel had said he sometimes makes her have anal sex he became angry. When he had calmed he admitted that he likes it that way sometimes.

  He said that he continues to masturbate most days, usually in the morning and thinks that Rachel knows that is what he does. She has not said anything and he believes that she does not mind.

He does not see himself as being physically attractive to the opposite sex but that does not cause him a problem because he knows that Rachel loves him and that is all that matters.

He does not want to be physically attractive to other men and certainly not to boys. He described himself as heterosexual.

He thinks his most sexually attractive feature is 'chatting women up'. He has sometimes found it difficult establishing new relationships as his anger has sometimes been an obstacle. He commented, 'Women need to realise that men get angry sometimes – it is the way we are made.'

He has never had sex with adults he did not know although he does not see sex as having to be part of a relationship. He agreed that he has never been offered casual sex except for his first sexual encounter. He has never gone to a prostitute or paid for sex.

John described himself as being sexually 'normal'. He has seen pornographic material in the past but that was many years ago.

He initially denied accessing pornographic material on the Internet until informed that the police had confiscated his computer. John admitted that he had viewed 'lots' of pornographic material and some child pornography. When this was further explored John said it was accessed accidentally but when this was challenged he admitted he was curious as some of his friends had talked about it. He refused to say who these friends were.

He sees the future as being bleak unless people agree that he is not a danger to children. If they do, he thinks he will move away from the area and start a new life somewhere else.

Issues arising from this information

- John's initial description of himself focused on his being a non-abusing adult.

- He reinforced the view that he is 'ordinary'.

- He indicates a different behaviour outside of the family home, helpful, amenable, friendly to the way he expresses himself at home.

- His feelings of anger and frustration at Adel and Rachel are clear as well as a general dissatisfaction with his life.

- He also reported stress as a significant issue at home.

- He presents himself as sexually heterosexual and 'normal'.

- He minimises the behaviour of Paul R.

- There is some evidence of confusion regarding people's sexual orientation.

- He was sexually embarrassed and humiliated as a teenager by his peers.

- The issue of whether or not he was sexually abused by Paul R remains unresolved but disclosure followed by retraction is not uncommon in children who have disclosed abuse.

- He reported being sexually active with his first partner Mary and he used angry/demanding behaviour when she refused him sex. Violence is also alleged within their relationship and the police reports would seem to confirm that.

- There is evidence that he insists on particular types of sexual activity even if his partner is not in agreement.

- He denied finding men or boys sexually attractive.

- He has accessed child pornography but only conceded this when evidence was presented to him. This should be seen as a sign that he is likely to deny other matters unless he feels he has no alternative but to do so, or is presented with undeniable evidence.

2.9 ADULT RELATIONSHIPS

When assessing adults who sexually abuse children it is important to understand the nature and character of the relationships they have with other adults. The nature of previous and current relationships gives significant insight into the behaviour of the adult and in particular informs about issues such as dominance, power and control, the extent to which adults are submissive and how they manage those relationships. Two distinct groups of adults are relevant.

- Adults about whom there are child protection concerns, specifically those involving the sexual abuse of children.

- Previous partners and the adult's current relationship, if applicable. This is particularly important in cases where the sexual abuse has occurred within the 'family'. Such information enables an understanding of the extent to which the non-abusing adult has actively or passively colluded with the abusing adult and their ability to be part of child protection and safe care arrangements.

Checklist for association with other adults about whom there are child protection concerns

1. What is the person's name?

2. How did you meet them?

3. How old were you both at the time?

4. What was happening in your life at the time?

5. What did you find attractive about them?

6. How long did the relationship last?

7. Describe them.

8. What did you like best about them?

9. Was there anything you disliked about them?

10. Describe your relationship.

11. Was there any violence shown towards you or any other person?

12. If so, describe what happened.

13. Were you ever violent towards that person?

14. If so, describe what happened.

15. Had they had previous relationships? If so, did they ever talk about them?

16. Did they have a criminal record?

17. Were any of the offences related to children? If so, do you know any of the details?

18. Do they have any friends/associates who have convictions for sex offences against children, or where there are child protection concerns?

19. What are the child protection concerns in respect of them?

20. What do you think about those child protection concerns?

21. Did you believe there was a risk to children?

22. Do you now believe the person to be a risk to children?

23. Why did your relationship end?

24. How did you feel about the relationship ending?

Case study

John's association with other adults

Re Paul R

John said that this was the most important relationship he has ever had. He met Paul R when he was eight and they remain friends, although John sees Paul R as a father figure. The only time they have been separated is when Paul R has been in prison for offences relating to the sexual abuse of children.

Paul R initially befriended John when he had run away from home to avoid a beating from his stepfather. He was very unhappy and enjoyed the attention which Paul R gave him.

John described Paul R as someone who has been accused of abusing children but he knows that not to be the case. When I asked how he knew that he replied, 'I would know by the look on their face.' When I asked what look and how would he know he was unable to elaborate but said he would know.

The thing he likes most about Paul R is the way he looked after him when he was small and has stood by him despite the most recent allegations. He does not like the way Paul R always wants young girls around him, especially ones who are not too clever.

He initially said that Paul R had never been violent towards him but when this was pursued he recalled an incident when he had gone into Paul R's bedroom to look for something and one of the young girls who was a frequent visitor saw him and reported the matter. Paul R had been very angry and had punched him in the face. He had witnessed Paul R being violent to the girls who visited but said that was because they wound him up and called him names. When asked he said they called him 'sugar daddy' and 'Paul the ponce'. When this was pursued he refused to accept that this was in any way connected to any sexual issues in respect of the girls. He became angry and refused to discuss the matter further.

John confirmed that Paul R had served two prison sentences for the sexual abuse of children but that he had not done anything to them. He said the girls had told lies about him. He did not know the details and did not want to know. He also confirmed that Paul R was on the sex offenders list and that he has been told by the social workers that he should have no contact with children. During a subsequent session, John admitted that he was currently living with Paul R.

John does not believe that Paul R presents a risk to children. When it was pointed out to him that he had said previously that he and a girl had been physically assaulted by Paul R in the past he said that was different, they had both deserved it.

They both have friends who have been convicted for offences against children and he pointed out that these were the only people who would now speak to him after Adel had told the lies about him.

He intends to continue his relationship with Paul R in the future.

Checklist for previous and present relationships

1. Beginning with your first serious relationship, what was the person's name?

2. How old were you both when you met?

3. What was happening in your life at the time?

4. How did you meet?

5. What attracted you to each other?

6. How long did the relationship last?

7. How long did you live together?

8. Describe the person.

9. What was the best thing about them?

10. What was the thing you least liked about them?

11. Describe your relationship, the things you did together.

12. Was he or she ever violent towards you?

13. Were you ever violent towards him or her?

14. Did the partner ever say things which hurt or upset you?

15. If so, what did they say and how often?

16. If you could change anything about that partner, what would it be?

17. If you could change anything about that relationship, what would it be?

18. Had there ever been any concerns about that partner's involvement with children?

19. Did they have any form of criminal record or had they been arrested for anything?

20. Did you have any children?

21. Were there any concerns about the children?

22. What happened to the children after you separated?

23. Why did your relationship end?

24. What do you feel about the relationship now?

Case study

John's previous relationships
Mary

John met Mary when he was 23 and she was 16. They met at Paul R's house, were together for 11 years and lived with Paul R during that time. John said they did not have any children. According to John, Mary had been sexually abused as a child and could not have children as a result of this. He said he did not exactly know who had abused her but thought it might have been her stepfather. He said it was nothing to do with him what had happened to her when she was a child.

He was first attracted to her because she was quiet, not like the other girls he had known. She did not drink and would do him favours, for example lend him money if he needed to buy some cigarettes.

He described her in the following terms:

'She did as she was told.'

'She sometimes made me angry when she would not do things.'

'She was a bit thick, you often had to tell her loads of times to do things.'

'Paul [Paul R] and me used to wind her up.'

'Paul [Paul R] used to play fight with her all the time.'

'In the end I got fed up with her.'

John did not disclose the domestic violence and when he was asked about this he became angry. He denied that he was violent towards Mary, apart from the 'odd slap when she was out of order'. He qualified 'out of order' as being when she did not do as she was told or if she moaned about something. When asked whether he thought it was right that he should hit Mary at all he replied, 'Why not, all men do it. Anyway she should not have made me angry.'

He said that he has no contact with her now – when they separated, the social workers arranged for her to go into a hostel somewhere away from Newtown.

John's present relationship
Rachel

John met Rachel when he was 35 and she was 15. They met at a local drop in centre. He explained that the centre was set up by the local community in a house on the estate. At the time they met Rachel was still living at home and was pregnant. John said she was unhappy and he felt sorry for her. They began to live together almost immediately; this was at the home of Paul R. He described her in the following terms:

'She is all right.'

'She can be really smart sometimes, other times she can be really stupid.'

'She forgets to do things sometimes, like keeping the house tidy.'

'She loves me.'

'She can be a bit annoying.'

'She is good with the kids, once I showed her how it should be done she was okay.'

'She wants to be with me and the kids.'

'She knows I haven't done anything to Adel, she knows Adel is a lying little bugger.'

'Sometimes she makes me lose my temper.'

After the birth of Adel he said things became difficult for a time. Rachel was not particularly good at looking after her and according to John he did most of the child care. They started having arguments and there were times when he lost his temper. He denied ever hitting her but said he had 'given her a good shaking sometimes'. He was asked whether or not he felt he had the right to physically abuse her in any way and he replied that 'shaking her was not the same as giving her a good slap'.

The thing he most likes about Rachel is that she does as she is told most of the time. The thing he least likes is when he has to keep reminding her to things, for example his tea is usually not ready on time. When it was suggested that these tasks could be shared he pointed out that he was responsible for sorting the kids out and Rachel had to look after the house and things.

He said that they spend most of their time together, usually visiting friends (these tend to be friends of John). They do not visit her family following a disagreement between them and John about five years ago. If he goes out alone, Rachel usually stays at home.

John believes that his relationship with Rachel will continue. He commented:

'She needs me.'

'I'm there to tell her what to do, otherwise she would be getting it all wrong.'

'She wouldn't get anybody to look after her better than me.'

'She knows she has it good with me.'

Issues arising from this information
Paul R

- This relationship has had a significant impact upon John's childhood and life experiences. The influence is both historical and current. Father figure, abuser, possibly co-abuser.

- It is likely that he knows much more about the abuse which Paul R perpetrated than he has revealed.

- His attitude to Paul R's offences shows his capacity for denial and minimisation.

- John's continued loyalty to him is of concern, as is their ongoing relationship.

Mary

- Mary was 16 years of age when they met.

- She was quiet, passive and compliant. She may have had a degree of learning disability. She was therefore vulnerable to exploitation.

- There is evidence of domestic violence which John sees as a legitimate part of their relationship. There is frequently a connection between domestic violence and child abuse.

- John was powerful and controlling within this relationship.

- Anger was also a feature within the relationship.

Rachel

- Rachel was only 15 years of age when they met and possibly started living together.

- He admits to lots of anger and temper within this relationship and this reinforces the notion that they are significant aspects of his behaviour.

- His concept of domestic violence is distorted and such cognitive distortion is part of the sexual abuse cycle.

- He expects Rachel to be compliant and he presumes a dominant role. He does not therefore see her as someone who is able to protect herself or her children from his behaviour.

- Rachel is isolated from her family and has no friends. Her only effective support system is John. Adults who sexually abuse children often create this isolation; it prevents outsiders from interfering and reinforces the dependency on them.

- John is confident that he has generated this dependency and convinced Rachel that he can look after her better than anyone else.

2.10 PERCEPTION OF CHILDREN OF THE 'FAMILY' (EXCLUDING THE VICTIM)

Gaining an understanding of the adult's perception of the children of the 'family' is crucial in:

- evaluating his or her emotional connection to them

- understanding any sexual interest he or she has in them

- identifying whether of not he or she has begun to groom them for sexual abuse

- establishing appropriate child protection arrangements for the child(ren).

Adults who have a negative attitude towards the child or are angry with the child may make that child more vulnerable to anger-motivated intra-familial abuse.

A particularly loving, tactile, idealised view of the child may indicate the child's vulnerability to being the victim of intra-familial abuse, as would a child who is described in physically attractive terms.

Checklist for perception of children of the 'family'

1. What is the child's name, age, date of birth?

2. What do you call him or her?

3. Where does the child live?

4. What is your relationship to the child?

5. How long have you known him or her?

6. How did you meet?

7. What does the child call you? (Dad, Father, by name?)

8. Describe the child. (Do not use the words physically or emotionally, allow the adult to decide the description. When they have finished prompt them on areas they have not described.)

9. Describe the thing you most like about them.

10. Describe the thing you least like about them.

11. Describe their behaviour.

12. Is there any behaviour which you feel unable to manage?

13. How do you think they would describe you?

14. What is the child's response to discipline?

15. Has he or she ever needed any form of medical attention?

16. Has he or she ever been seen by a doctor for anything involving her vagina/his penis or his or her anus?

17. Has he or she ever been to a hospital for anything involving her vagina/his penis or his or her anus?

18. Do you think they have been abused in any way?

19. What would you do if you thought anyone was abusing them in any way?

Case study

John's responses to the checklist for children of the 'family'

Stephanie

Stephanie is five years old and is John's eldest daughter. He calls her Steph. They lived together until he was asked to leave the family home following the disclosure by Adel. She calls him Dad. He described her in the following terms:

'She is skinny.'

'She used to do as she was told but she is getting like Adel.'

'She knows not to cross me – I make her do as she is told.'

'She can be cheeky.'

'She always wants things.'

'She is always moaning her friends have things, why can't she have them, does she think I am made of money?'

'She won't do as her mother says.'

He likes her most when she behaves like Jasmine and least when she is acting like Adel.

John said that Stephanie had been to the doctor for the usual illnesses and infections. During one visit to the doctor some soreness was noted around her anus but John said that she scratched a lot and was often constipated. He said she was sore quite often.

He is convinced Stephanie has not been abused in any way. He said he would know if anyone had done anything to her. When asked how he would know he was unable to elaborate other than to repeat he would know.

If he thought anyone was abusing Stephanie he would put a stop to it. He was unable to say how he would do this but when asked specifically he did not exclude violence as a response.

Jasmine

Jasmine is three years old; she is John's child. He calls her 'my little angel'. She calls him Daddy. He described her in the following terms:

'She is beautiful.'

'She is so pretty.'

'She loves me, I love her.'

'She really likes being tickled.'

'She does as she is told straight away.'

'She likes being with me – she hates it when I go out.'

He likes everything about her and dislikes nothing. He described her behaviour as perfect.

Jasmine has never been to the doctor or hospital for any issues involving her anus or vagina.

He finally commented that if anyone abused her he would kill them.

Issues arising from this information

Stephanie

- John sees Stephanie as an unattractive, disobedient child.

- His comparison with Adel is worrying and might indicate the emergence of a similar response from him. His comments might be seen as part of his cognitive distortions.

- There is already evidence of his anger towards her and anger is a significant feature in his abusive cycle.

- Her anus is frequently sore and although there is currently no evidence to support sexual abuse, professionals should be alert to the possibility.

Jasmine

- She is seen as a physically attractive child.

- Their relationship is very special to him and the issue of 'intra-familial abuse' should be an ongoing consideration.

2.11 CRIMINAL HISTORY – NON-SEXUAL OFFENCES

Practitioners should explore the adult's criminal history, and the following issues are of particular interest:

- the circumstances of the offences

- the nature of the offences

- offences of violence or where violence was involved

- sentences received and their benefit or otherwise.

Some determination may be required from practitioners. Adults sometimes challenge the relevance of such information and are reluctant to go into the details. Others say they do not remember the details of the offences. Practitioners should also explore any incident where charges were preferred but the matter was not proceeded with.

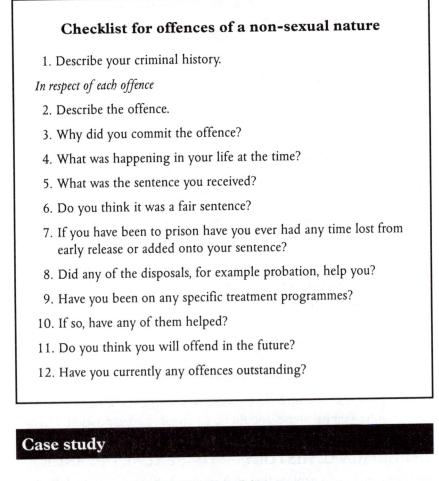

Checklist for offences of a non-sexual nature

1. Describe your criminal history.

In respect of each offence

2. Describe the offence.

3. Why did you commit the offence?

4. What was happening in your life at the time?

5. What was the sentence you received?

6. Do you think it was a fair sentence?

7. If you have been to prison have you ever had any time lost from early release or added onto your sentence?

8. Did any of the disposals, for example probation, help you?

9. Have you been on any specific treatment programmes?

10. If so, have any of them helped?

11. Do you think you will offend in the future?

12. Have you currently any offences outstanding?

Case study

John's non-sexual offending history

John explained that he had a number of convictions for criminal damage when he was a teenager. He said that he would get really angry and 'just lash out at things'.

Afterwards he said that he felt better. At the time he was either living with Paul R or at home. The incidents of criminal damage to his mother's home always occurred when he was not living there and would usually be throwing bricks through her windows. He would often spray his name on the buildings he had vandalised and he knew the police would come for him. That would make him angry again and he would 'struggle' when they arrested him. He was initially given a conditional discharge, then fines, which his mother refused to pay, and eventually probation orders. He said that all of the disposals were 'useless'. In particular the probation officer would want him to talk about his feelings and his relationship with his mother and he felt that was a waste of time. 'No one helped me, they were there to sort things out, but they didn't.'

At 19 years of age, John was convicted of an assault on a 14-year-old girl. At the time he was living with Paul R. She was a girl he knew because she visited Paul R's house. John said that she was 'really cheeky, she would be smart with her mouth all the time'. She had made fun of John from time to time and he had 'slapped her a bit'. He said that on the occasion of the offence she had 'really wound me up'. He remembered her laughing at him and calling him a 'puff'. He initially said he was unable to recall the details, then said he had given her 'a good slap'. He was asked why, if he had only hit her once, she had reported him on this occasion when she had not previously done so. He said he did not know. It was put to him that the sentence (two years' probation and attendance at an anger management course) suggested much more than a single slap. He accepted that he may have hit her more than once. He had lost his temper and could not remember how many times he had hit her. He said it was her fault; she should not have 'wound him up'.

John was asked about the anger management. He said it was a waste of time. He was asked if he recalled any of the details. He said they talked about 'triggers' and 'strategies' but he had not really listened. He said he had only attended because the court said he would go to prison if he did not attend.

The offence of street robbery was against a ten-year-old boy and involved the theft of some money. At the time he was living in a bedsit or maybe at home. He was vague about the details but insisted that he did not hit the boy. It was pointed out that the offence indicated a level of violence and he said that he might have threatened to 'punch his lights out', unless he gave him the money. He said that when he was in prison he attended an anger management course, but only because he was told it would qualify him for an earlier release. He lost some time for fighting. He said that he and some of the other prisoners 'beat up a puff'.

Issues arising from this information

- Anger, particularly against his mother, featured in his early life and is likely to remain unresolved.

- The offence of violence against the 14-year-old girl further supports the notion that he sees physical violence as a legitimate problem-solving device and has no reservations about using violence against women.

- The offence of street robbery also indicates a level of violence, raising the issue of his potential to use it against those he perceives to be weaker than himself.

2.12 DRUGS AND ALCOHOL

Drugs and alcohol are known to act as internal disinhibitors (Finklehor 1986) and it is therefore important that practitioners collect all necessary information. Where there is a level of misuse, the connection of this to behaviour should be considered in detail.

Checklist for drugs and alcohol

1. If you have used drugs, when did you begin?

2. Why did you start taking drugs?

3. Are you still taking drugs? If so, what?

4. Who introduced you to drugs?

5. Describe your use of drugs up to the current time.

6. Have you ever been on a 'drug treatment' programme?

7. If so, what happened?

8. How do the drugs make you feel?

9. Does your behaviour change when you have taken drugs?

10. If so, in what way?

11. Does your partner know about your drug habit?

12. If so, what does he or she say about it?

Repeat the questions in respect of alcohol use

Case study

John's use of drugs and alcohol

John said he has never used any of the hard 'drugs because that is for mugs'. He did smoke heroin on a few occasions when he was in his early twenties but it made him feel sick and did not give him the buzz everyone said it would.

He started drinking when he was about 14 years old. He said Paul R had always been a binge drinker and John sometimes joined him. There were times when he would get so drunk he could not remember things the next day. Since then he has been a regular drinker and at times he gets drunk. The last occasion had been the previous weekend; he said it was a response to all the pressure he was under. He acknowledged that 'he drinks socially most days' and usually gets drunk once a week. He does not see his alcohol use as a problem; he believes that he drinks no more than most of the men who live locally. He initially denied that alcohol changed his mood but following a discussion he accepted that he is more likely to lose his temper when he has been drinking. He denied that any of the incidents between him and Rachel were the result of his drinking.

Issues arising from this information

- Drugs do not appear to feature in his lifestyle and living arrangements.

- Alcohol does feature. It acts as a disinhibitor to his management of his anger and probably to other aspects of his behaviour.

- His comment that he has never been physically abusive to Rachel when he has been drinking is unlikely to be true.

2.13 SELF-ESTEEM

The initial part of the assessment was based upon the adult's self-report, and included their concept of themselves, their relationships and their understanding of the events in their lives. Whilst some of those reports may and should have been challenged when that was appropriate, specific areas need to be visited or revisited to gain a precise understanding of aspects of behaviour which relate directly to the sexual abuse of children.

An adult's self-esteem informs the general level of confidence they have, their concept of their skills and abilities and the extent to which they feel competent. People with a good level of self-esteem can achieve things, feel good about themselves and are usually well motivated. This is important if change is required or new skills need to be developed.

People with a low self-esteem have little confidence in themselves, find change more difficult and are not generally motivated to develop new skills.

It is significant in the assessment of adults who sexually abuse children as a low self-esteem is one of the factors present in some cases.

It is also significant in gaining an understanding of the partner or other adult carer's ability to protect the child from further abuse.

The score recorder should be compared to the level at which the practitioner estimates the self-esteem to be from a review of all of the work with the adult. Significant differences may be worthy of further investigation or could indicate a false report.

The checklist below looks at different areas of self-esteem:

- the adult's concept of themselves physically and sexually

- the adult's perception of their skills, abilities, confidence and self-worth

- the adult's perception of how they believe other people see them

- their relationship with the 'outside world' (those arrangements outside of their personal, interpersonal and close social relationships).

The 'O' is a self-esteem positive and scores 2 points; the '□' is a self-esteem negative and scores 0; the '△' scores 1 point. A person's self-esteem is probably in the good range if two-thirds of the answers are in the positive or a score of 48 is achieved. However, the score should not be seen as a rigid measure. It should be compared to the practitioner's evaluation of the adult's self-esteem throughout the assessment sessions and adjusted accordingly. If the adult responds with the neutral answer 'don't know' too frequently the practitioner needs to consider that the checklist is being compromised and challenge this. Too many 'don't knows' may also indicate a high level of personal uncertainty and this will suggest a low self-esteem.

- The adult's concept of themselves physically and sexually is indicated by their answers to questions: 13, 22, 28, 29, 30, 33.

- The adult's perception of their skills, abilities, confidence and self-worth is indicated by their answers to questions: 1, 2, 3, 4, 5, 6, 7, 10, 11, 12, 15, 16, 17, 21, 23, 26, 27, 31, 32, 34, 35, 36.

- The adult's perception of how they believe other people see them is indicated by their answers to questions: 9, 14, 18, 24, 25.

- The adult's relationship with the 'outside world' (those arrangements outside of their personal, interpersonal and close social relationships) is indicated by their answers to questions: 8, 19, 20.

Checklist for self-esteem

	Yes	No	Don't Know
1. Do you feel you can do things as well as other people?	O	□	△
2. Do you have things you are proud of?	O	□	△
3. Do you often feel you are a failure?	□	O	△
4. Do you think you are as good as other people?	O	□	△
5. Are there a lot of things about yourself you would change?	□	O	△
6. Do you often wish you were someone else?	□	O	△
7. Do you think you are a confident person?	O	□	△
8. Do you feel uncomfortable when you are with people you have not met before?	□	O	△
9. Do you think other people like you?	O	□	△
10. Do you sometimes feel useless?	□	O	△
11. Do you have confidence in your decisions?	O	□	△
12. Do you have a good opinion of yourself?	O	□	△
13. Do you like having your photograph taken?	□	O	△

	Yes	No	Don't Know
14. Are there family members who do not like you?	☐	○	△
15. Do you get upset if someone criticises you?	☐	○	△
16. Do you think people regard you as being useless?	☐	○	△
17. Do you feel ashamed of things you have done?	☐	○	△
18. Do you find it hard to believe people who say nice things about you?	☐	○	△
19. Do you sometimes remain silent because you think people might laugh at what you have to say?	☐	○	△
20. Are you shy in large groups?	☐	○	△
21. Do you feel you can succeed in doing things you want to?	○	☐	△
22. Are you happy with the way you look?	○	☐	△
23. Do you feel you do things right most of the time?	○	☐	△
24. Do you think that people will not like you?	☐	○	△
25. Do you find people telling you that you have done things the wrong way?	☐	○	△
26. Do you ever pretend to be better at things than you really are?	☐	○	△
27. Do you sometimes feel you can never do anything right?	☐	○	△
28. Do you think you are physically attractive?	○	☐	△
29. Do you think you are sexually attractive?	○	☐	△
30. Do you think you are a good sexual partner?	○	☐	△
31. Do you have a normal amount of respect for yourself?	○	☐	△

32. Do you think you have a good personality?	○	□	△
33. Do you feel that sometimes your sexual performance is not as good as you would like it to be?	□	○	△
34. Do you think you are a success as a person?	○	□	△
35. Are there things you would have liked to have achieved but have not?	□	○	△
36. Would you like to be able to do things better than you can?	□	○	△

Case study

John's self-esteem

John's self-esteem was recorded as being in the good range. He showed a good level of confidence in his skills and abilities and has a good concept of himself physically and sexually. He has some reservation about how other people see him, particularly since Adel's disclosure, and his self-esteem is not good in respect of his interactions with the outside world.

Issues arising from this information

- John's self-esteem indicates he is a confident person at home but not when he is in the community.

2.14 DOMINANT AND SUBMISSIVE BEHAVIOUR

The extent to which power is exercised and adults are compliant with dominant adults can be a vital part of the assessment. This is particularly the case when we are considering the 'family unit', as this is where child protection and the sexual abuse of children are most frequently found.

A dominant disposition can inform the sexually abusive behaviour, either as an exercise of that power or when attempts to exercise dominance are resisted and/or resented. Understanding that can therefore add significantly to the assessment information.

Conversely, submissive and compliant behaviour gives clues to the extent to which that person can be dominated, manipulated or controlled. This is particularly important when looking at the adult's partner or the other adult carer. Submissive/compliant people have difficulty in protecting themselves and any other person for whom they have responsibility, including children. Submissive/compliant people are not connected to anger-motivated intra-familial abuse.

Checklist for dominant/submissive behaviour

1. Would you describe yourself as a confident person?

   all the time   most of the time   some of the time   none of the time

2. Where do you feel most confident?

3. Do you believe you are someone who likes to be in control of situations?

   all the time   most of the time   some of the time   none of the time

4. Are you someone who lacks confidence?

   all the time   most of the time   some of the time   none of the time

5. Do you rely on other people?

   all the time   most of the time   some of the time   none of the time

6. What kind of things do you rely on them for?

7. If you thought you were in the right would you argue with people?

   all the time   most of the time   some of the time   none of the time

8. Who do you argue with most?

9. Why that person?

10. What are the arguments about?

11. Who usually wins those arguments?

12. Do you expect people to do as you say?

   all the time   most of the time   some of the time   none of the time

---

13. Do you think you are nervous?

   all the time   most of the time   some of the time   none of the time

14. What kind of things make you feel nervous?

15. What would you do if people do not do as you say?

16. What would you do if your partner does not do as you say?

17. What would you do if the children do not do as you say?

18. What do you do if people try to take over when you are doing something and you know you are right?

19. Are you stubborn?

   all the time   most of the time   some of the time   none of the time

20. Do you get your own way?

   all the time   most of the time   some of the time   none of the time

21. Do you like to get your own way?

   all the time   most of the time   some of the time   none of the time

22. Does anyone else make important decisions for you?

23. Do you make important decisions by yourself?

24. Do you insist that people apologise to you if they are in the wrong?

25. What do you do if they do not apologise to you?

26. Do you sometimes become angry with people to make your point?

27. Have you ever pretended to be angry to frighten people?

28. Have you ever pretended to be angry to get your own way?

29. Do you think showing emotions is a sign of weakness?

30. Do you think crying is a sign of weakness?

Case study

John's responses to the dominant/submissive behaviour checklist

John sees himself as a confident person most of the time. He feels most confident when he is at home. He likes to be in control of situations all of the time and manages that at home except for the behaviour of Adel. He only lacks confidence when he is in unfamiliar social situations and avoids these as much as possible.

He only relies on Paul R and then only some of the time. He has been advised by him about what to say and do following the allegations made against him by Adel.

If he felt he was in the right he would say what he thought but would not usually get into an argument. He would argue with people who were accusing him of things he had not done and if anyone was picking on Rachel or the kids and he disagreed with what they were saying.

He argues most with Rachel because she keeps doing things wrong and that annoys him. They argue 'about everything', and he always wins.

He feels people do not do as he says when he is outside but at home they do, except for Adel.

He said he is not a nervous person but can be nervous when he is in unfamiliar situations, for example when he has to go to court.

Rachel always does as he says, 'eventually', although when they first started to live together he had to threaten her sometimes before she did as she was told.

He said the children know better than to disregard his instructions, except for Adel who he feels winds him up so that he loses his temper. He said that he shouts at her until she does as she is told. He said that he had never hit her.

He does not like it when people try to take over and it depends on the circumstances as to his response. When this was explored he said that at home he will stop them from interfering but outside he will usually let other people get on with it.

He accepts that he can be stubborn and he makes his own decisions, except that he sometimes talks to Paul R.

He can become angry with people and has pretended to be angry in the past so that people would not try to take advantage of him.

He thinks crying and showing emotions is a sign of weakness.

Issues arising from this information

- This confirms his good level of confidence within the home and lack of confidence outside.

- John is dominant at home but may be compliant/submissive in his relationship with Paul R.

- A dominant relationship is indicated with Rachel and a level of coercion is evident.

- The negative concept of Adel is again apparent. His comment that he has never hit her is at variance with her disclosure and this could be further explored.

- He confirms that he uses anger as a tool to prevent people 'taking advantage of him'. He also appears to use it to prevent people from exploring potentially difficult areas of his behaviour, concepts and belief systems.

2.15 ANGRY, AGGRESSIVE AND VIOLENT BEHAVIOUR

One of the main issues to be considered by practitioners is that of the relationship between anger and the sexual abuse of children.

In particular there is a direct connection between domestic violence and sexual abuse and this should be explored throughout the assessment sessions. This is particularly important where the adult who has sexually abused the child wants to return to the family home and there are known to have been issues and domestic violence previously.

Anger leads to violence and violence is part of the sexual abuse process. When adults become angry with children their impulse controls are likely to be reduced and their internal inhibitors are overcome.

People who are the victims of violence have their physical and emotional wellbeing compromised. They feel fear, isolation and despair. They are unable to protect themselves and those for whom they have responsibility, including children. This is particularly relevant in the case of partners or the adult carers of children who have been sexually abused.

It is known that there is a direct connection between domestic violence and sexual abuse. The relationship between the adult who has sexually abused the child and the non-abusing parent should be specifically explored as should domestic violence in previous relationships.

This checklist presumes that the adult has angry feelings which need to be explored. The adult's denial that they do not have angry feelings should be challenged and the checklist applied. Although a submissive partner may also deny having angry feelings that will not necessarily be the case and the checklist should also be applied to them. At the time this checklist is applied the information from the earlier sessions can be used in support of questions, as an example to the adult that they do have anger issues. For example, in the case study information is already available that John has been angry with and physically abused Rachel and his answers can be connected to some of those episodes to confirm the nature of his anger and also to identify his triggers.

It may be helpful to remind practitioners at this stage that adults are generally reluctant to discuss issues of anger and violence, particularly if they are wanting to present themselves in a positive light and the following features may need to be considered:

- the probability/possibility of minimisation

- detail may be under-reported or forgotten (selective memory)

- denial, either absolute or partial

- hostility or refusal. (If hostility is encountered, this could well be an angry response, part of a strategy to avoid discussion or a 'dominance' response designed to put the practitioners off a particular issue; this should be explored with the adult. If it is felt, however, to be a 'defence mechanism' response it should be explored accordingly.)

The checklist for angry behaviour looks at two key areas of anger:

- those situations in which anger is felt

- the emotions felt by the adult during these periods of anger.

Checklist for angry/aggressive behaviour

1. Are you an angry person?

   all the time   most of the time   some of the time   none of the time

2. How often do you become angry with yourself?

   all the time   most of the time   some of the time   none of the time

3. How often do you become angry with other people?

   all the time   most of the time   some of the time   none of the time

4. How often do you become angry with your partner?

   all the time   most of the time   some of the time   none of the time

5. How often did you become angry with (name of child victim)?

   all the time   most of the time   some of the time   none of the time

6. When you are away from your home how often do you become angry?

   all the time   most of the time   some of the time   none of the time

7. What do you do if you feel angry away from home?

8. Who is the person you are most angry with?

9. Why do you think this is the case?

10. Are there any other people you are angry with a lot?

11. Are there any groups of people or organisations with whom you are angry?

12. Describe how you feel when you are getting angry.

13. Describe how you feel when you become angry.

14. Do you have any physical symptoms when you become angry (for example feeling hot)?

15. What do you do when you feel yourself losing your temper?

16. Does your anger build up until you explode?

17. Do you lash out at people when you are angry?

    all the time   most of the time   some of the time   none of the time

18. When you become angry do you feel you are about to lose control?

19. Do you become angry very quickly or do you have a slow fuse?

20. Do you feel ashamed of yourself if you have been angry?

21. Do you let people know you are angry so they won't try to push you about?

22. Do you find anger motivates you to get things done?

23. When you are angry do you find it difficult to think straight?

24. When you are angry does it prevent you from thinking about anything else?

25. Does anger make you feel helpless and frustrated?

26. Do you keep your anger bottled up inside you?

27. Does your anger lead to aggression?

    all the time   most of the time   some of the time   none of the time

28. Are you able to control your anger?

    all the time   most of the time   some of the time   none of the time

29. Give an example of when you controlled your behaviour.

30. Is it okay to feel angry if you can control it?

31. Do you feel powerful when you are angry?

32. Does anger give you a feeling of energy?

33. Do you hate yourself when you have been angry?

    all the time   most of the time   some of the time   none of the time

34. Do you feel anger is a waste of energy?

35. Do you feel ashamed of yourself if people have seen you angry?

36. Do you think a child's anger is bad and needs to be punished?

37. Do you prefer to keep your anger to yourself?

38. Do you feel your anger is a problem?

39. If so what would you like to do about it?

40. Have you ever attended an anger management course?

41. If so, what did it achieve for you?

42. Do you think you are an angry person?

43. If so, why do you think you are an angry person?

44. Do you use anger to dominate people?

45. Do you use anger to stop people getting too close to you?

46. Do you think anger is a good thing or a bad thing?

It is possible to revisit the above questions looking at the issue of aggression rather than anger.

Case study

John's angry/aggressive behaviour

John feels he was an angry person most of the time when he was at home with Rachel and the children. He did not become angry with himself but mainly with Rachel and Adel. Towards the end he was angry at least once every day.

When he is out of the home he does not feel angry very often, but even when he does he prefers to keep his angry feelings to himself. He does this to avoid trouble with other people.

He is most angry with Adel and nearly as angry with Rachel for letting Adel get away with the things she did.

He thinks that he has angry feelings 'bubbling away all of the time', but then something will happen which makes the anger rise to the surface. When he is angry he feels quite powerful, full of energy. He likes to shout a lot when he is angry. Outside of the home he is able to control any angry feelings he has, but at home he just lets them come out. He said that if he had to control his anger at home he would 'burst'.

There have been times in the past when he has lashed out at Rachel but he said he has never hit Adel. He was asked why his response was different when the angry feelings were just as intense. He replied that he knows you should not hit children. It was then suggested to John that this indicated he could either manage his anger when he chose to or he was not being truthful. He said he was telling the truth.

He said he did not have any particular physical symptoms when he became angry.

When he is away from home he walks away from any situation which is causing him anger. At home he does not walk away and commented, 'Why should I? It's my house.'

He does not feel ashamed of becoming angry and feels that it is not his fault. If Adel would do as she is told and Rachel would not wind him up and argue all of the time he would not become angry.

He attended an anger management course when he was in prison, aged 19. He described this as a waste of time because all they did was to talk about his childhood and why that would make him angry. He said it was not his childhood which made him angry; it was all the questions they kept asking him and the way they wanted to interfere in and control his life.

He denied that he used anger to dominate people but accepted that when he became angry Rachel did as she was told immediately and Adel became 'less stroppy and awkward'.

Issues arising from this information

- Anger features regularly for John. It is projected outwards within the context of his family. He does not blame himself for his anger; he blames others.

- He may not be overall an angry person.

- He is specifically angry at Adel and this raises the question of anger motivated intra-familial abuse.

- A previous anger management course was not helpful to him and he does not have a positive attitude towards such intervention.

Checklist for violent behaviour

1. Are you a violent person?

   all the time   most of the time   some of the time   none of the time

2. Are you more likely to be violent if you have been drinking?

3. What is the most violent thing you have done?

4. Describe your last violent incident.

5. How many times have you been violent in the past?

6. Can you imagine yourself being violent in the future?

7. If not, what would you do differently in the future if the same circumstances arose?

8. If someone was annoying you would you hit them?

9. If someone hit you would you hit them back?

10. Have you ever wanted to really hurt another person?

11. Do you think hitting people is acceptable in certain circumstances?

12. If yes, what would those circumstances be?

13. Have you ever smashed things in the house when you have lost your temper?

14. If so, why do you think you did that?

15. Have you ever harmed yourself when you have lost your temper?

16. If so, why do you think you did that?

17. Did you get involved in fights when you were growing up?

18. Were you a bully when you were growing up?

19. Do you think you are a bully now?

20. Do you think you are violent?

    all the time   most of the time   some of the time   none of the time

Domestic violence

21. Have you ever been violent towards your previous partner(s)?

22. If so, how often and under what circumstances?

23. Have you ever been violent towards your current partner?

24. If so, under what circumstances?

25. Why?

26. How often?

27. Do you believe violence towards your partner was justified?

28. Have you and your partner ever talked about why you become violent?

29. If so what did you discuss and what did you decide?

30. Do you think domestic violence played any part in the sexual abuse of the child(ren)?

Case study

John's violent behaviour

John said he is not someone who is violent but when people wind him up he can become violent sometimes.

The most violent thing he has ever done is when he resisted arrest as a teenager and assaulted the police. He said it was their fault – if they had left him alone the assaults would not have occurred.

He said he is not violent very often. The last time was with Rachel just after Adel had accused him of abusing her. He said he had been drinking and this was why he lost his temper but Rachel had also been going on about whether or not he had touched Adel.

He thought he would not be violent in the future unless someone did something to wind him up. When specifically asked he said he would not be violent away from home as this only brought problems for him.

He has never harmed himself, was bullied by some children when he was small but got his revenge on them when he got older.

He believes he is violent about the same as other people but would be less so if people did not wind him up all the time.

He accepts that from time to time he has been violent towards Rachel but only when she has wound him up about something or she has not done as she has been told by him. He does not think that will change in the future.

Issues arising from this information

- This confirms the view that John does not see his behaviour as his fault or responsibility.

- He is always likely to minimise the extent of his violence.

- Violence is only evident within the family home.

- Domestic violence has been a feature in their relationship and he believes it will continue in the future.

2.16 THE ADULT'S PERCEPTION OF CHILD SEXUAL ABUSE

The extent to which the adult is able to look at the abuse from the child's perspective will provide information about:

- the process used by the adult to sexually abuse the child

- the extent to which he or she has been able to reflect on matters.

Adults are likely to want to present themselves in a positive light and practitioners should be aware of this tendency. Spontaneous answers are more likely to be a true reflection of how the adult thinks and feels. Pauses and apparent rehearsal should be treated with some suspicion and consideration should be given to revisiting the issue at some later time from a slightly different angle. Practitioners should also be aware that the adult may have already been asked similar questions previously and have some familiarity with the process. If that is the case practitioners should consider a more assertive approach to the questions.

Repeat perpetrators are more likely to be familiar with the process. Adults who have undertaken a Sex Offender Treatment Programme (SOTP) are likely to be familiar with the process of assessment and have some of the 'required answers' already available to them.

The practitioner should make it clear to the adult that 'don't know' is not an acceptable answer.

If 'maybe' and 'sometimes' is the answer, the practitioner should ask for elaboration or clarification.

The adult should be encouraged to answer the questions as quickly as possible.

If subsidiary questions arise from the answers, consider pursuing these immediately as this often adds to the quality of the information collected.

An analysis of the information provided in this checklist will indicate to the practitioner the adult's thinking, concepts and belief systems about the sexual abuse of children. Some of the questions revisit earlier issues and should be cross-referenced for honesty and accuracy.

There are groups of questions which address specific aspects of abuse although some of these areas overlap and practitioners should be prepared to look in 'overview' as well as within the specific areas shown below. The numbers of questions are referenced to the specific area.

Child protection and sexual abuse
3, 4, 32, 34, 36, 40, 41, 42, 43, 45

Adult's belief systems
5, 6, 7, 15, 17, 18, 23, 24, 35, 39, 59, 50, 51, 52

Adult's concept of age and sexual abuse
9, 10, 11, 12, 13, 14, 19, 20, 21, 22

Cognitive distortions
8, 15, 16, 25, 26, 27, 28, 30, 31, 44, 46, 47, 48

Understanding of the child's understanding of sexual matters
29, 33, 37, 38

Checklist for the adult's concepts about sexual abuse

1. Explain what you understand by the sexual abuse of children.

2. What kind of things do you think constitute sexual abuse?

3. Do you think that children should be protected from sexual abuse?

4. If so, how do you think that can be achieved?

5. Do you think sexually abusing children is right or wrong?

6. If you think it is right, why?

7. If you think it is wrong, why?

8. Is sexual contact with children by adults okay if the adult is gentle?

9. Is having sexual contact with a child of six years okay?

10. If so, why?

11. Is sexual contact with a child of 12 years okay?

12. If so, why?

13. Is sexual contact with a teenager of 14 years okay?

14. If so, why?

15. If the child touches you is that different to if you touch them?

16. If a teenager of 14 years has had sex before and agrees to sex with you what would you do?

17. If sex with children is not okay is it okay to touch each other's sexual parts?

18. If yes, why?

19. What do you think the age of sexual consent for girls should be?

20. If below 16 years, why do you think that?

21. Should the age of sexual consent be the same for boys and girls?

22. If yes, why?

23. Do you think society has the wrong attitude to sexual contact with children?

24. If so, why?

25. Do you think that some adults only have sex with children because they love them?

What do you think about the following comments?

26. Sexual activity with children does not harm them in any way unless you penetrate them.

27. Sexual activity with children does not harm them even if you do penetrate them.

28. Girls are ready for sex as soon as they start having periods.

29. Do you think children under ten years know what sex is about?

30. It is not against the law for children to have sex in some Eastern countries. What do you think about that statement?

31. Sexual contact with children is a good way of teaching them sex education.

32. Children should not be made to have sex with adults.

33. It is okay for children to have sex with each other.

34. Not enough is done to protect children from being sexually abused.

35. The sexual abuse of children by adults is on the increase.

36. Not enough is done to help children who have been sexually abused.

37. Some children lead adults on sexually.

38. Some children lead adults on – they deserve all they get.

39. Do you think that children are mainly abused by people who know them?

40. A child saying they have been sexually abused should not be believed just because they say they have.

41. If not, why not?

42. Women hardly ever abuse children sexually.

43. Only a certain type of man sexually abuses children.

44. Children over five years old would not be harmed if the adult is gentle.

45. Girls and boys are affected in the same way if they are sexually abused.

46. Masturbation of a child by an adult will cause them no harm.

47. Masturbation of an adult by a child will cause them no harm.

48. If children lead adults on sexually, it's okay.

49. Have you ever discussed with anyone else their understanding of sexual abuse of children?

50. Does your partner think the same way as you on matters of sexual abuse?

51. If yes, why?

52. If no, why?

Case study

John's concepts about sexual abuse

John explained that he had previously thought the sexual abuse of children involved having sex with them against their wishes. If they became upset that was not necessarily sexual abuse as Rachel sometimes became upset when they were having sex and that was not abusive. He had previously thought abuse was full sexual intercourse but now accepts that it involves any sexual contact with the child. He believes that children should be protected from sexual abuse and that can be done by explaining to them that if anything happens to them they do not like they should tell someone.

He said that he and Paul R had discussed the issues 'loads of times'.

He said that children should not be sexually abused. They should not have things happen to them they do not want, although he feels that some children want to have sex and that should be allowed. He said that some children 'ask for it because of their behaviour, they flaunt themselves at men'. Other children say no when they do not really mean it. He thinks that is the same with adult women.

He feels that the age of the child is not important as long as they do not object to having sex. Children are old enough to have sex much sooner than they used to be. John has seen children simulating sex at a very young age; he thinks that Stephanie and Jasmine (his children with Rachel) were doing it. He feels there should not be an age limit for consensual sex.

He said that when adults are 'play fighting' with children their sexual parts are sometimes touched but this is accidental. So long as no harm is done to the child then the behaviour is not abusive. He commented, 'Some children don't even know they are being touched up'.

He concluded, 'As long as no harm is done it's okay.'

He then reiterated that he had not intentionally sexually abused Adel, except on one occasion when he was bathing her. He said, 'Everyone is entitled to make one mistake'; he had learned his lesson and would not do it again.

Note   An analysis of the information will show if the adult has a distorted concept of matters which legitimises or supports their abusive behaviour. Conversely the adult may respond in a way which indicates that children should be protected from child sexual abuse, that they are not able to make decisions about such matters and that sexual abuse causes children significant harm.

Practitioners should be prepared for adults to report concepts and belief systems which indicate an entirely healthy and non-abusive attitude to the sexual abuse of children. Such a report should be viewed with a degree of scepticism and can be challenged.

One or more of the following further questions is likely to be appropriate.

Follow-up questions about the adult's concepts about sexual abuse

1. What has changed in your thinking since you sexually abused the child?

2. You have responded in a way which indicates you are not someone inclined towards the sexual abuse of children. Why then did you sexually abuse the child?

3. Do you believe that your views are the same as most adults or not?

4. If not, why not?

5. Would you like to change your thinking about the sexual abuse of children?

6. If not, why not?

7. Has your view of child sexual abuse changed since the child's disclosure?

8. Has your view of sexual abuse of children changed during the assessment?

Case study

John's responses to the further questions on his concept of the sexual abuse of children

John reiterated that he had only touched Adel inappropriately on one occasion.

He said that he had not really changed what he thought about children but now recognised that other people have said it was wrong. He does not believe it is wrong.

Issues arising from this information

- John refers to an increased understanding of child sexual abuse.

- However, his main adult discussion about such matters has been with Paul R, a known sex offender, and this is of significant concern. Paul R is most likely to have developed a range of cognitive distortions and defence mechanisms to protect himself.

- John's concepts are distorted; for example, he believes children have the ability to give informed consent.

- His responses are extremely worrying. He places no age limit on a child's agreement to sex. He believes that some children encourage sexual contact because of their behaviour. Verbal resistance is not seen by him to necessarily mean 'no'.

- John's responses to the 'further' questions is very worrying. He has not changed his concepts and belief systems in any way.

2.17 THE SEXUAL ABUSE OF THE CHILD(REN)

Having examined the adult's concepts and belief systems about the sexual abuse of children, the practitioner needs to look in detail at the adult's perpetrator-specific abusive behaviour. Where there is more than one conviction or where previous allegations have been made it may be most helpful to deal with them in historical sequence, as this may give clues to the development/evolution of the abusive behaviour. It may also identify, for example, how the 'grooming' process has been refined or made more sophisticated.

As with other parts of the assessment, denial, minimisation and failure to remember details are likely to feature and this should be challenged. Adults who sexually abuse children often use the abusive episodes as part of subsequent masturbation fantasy and therefore retain vivid memories of what has happened. It is sometimes appropriate to point out to the adult that a full understanding of the abuse is essential to inform the implementation of essential child protection plans. Without these, the adult's return to the family home may not be possible or the return of the child or other children to the family home may not occur.

There are two different ways of doing this:

- A free narrative account can be taken to see if the adult is giving an honest account of the sexual abuse. This will give an indication of the extent of any false report or cognitive distortions. The account can then be challenged and revisited using available information.

- Point out to the adult that information from court records, child protection case conferences and video disclosure interviews of the child have been accessed. In this way the adult recognises that information is already known and is more likely to give a more detailed account of the abusive episodes.

Checklist for the sexual abuse of the child(ren)

Deal with each episode / allegation / conviction separately

1. What was the child's name and age?
2. Describe the child.
3. How did you meet him or her?
4. How did you get to know him or her?
5. When was the first time you felt attracted to him or her?
6. When did you decide you were going to sexually abuse the child?
7. Describe what happened the first time you were alone with the child.
8. Describe the feelings you had for the child.
9. Describe the sexual feelings you had for the child.
10. Why did you want to sexually abuse the child?
11. How did you get him or her ready for the sexual abuse?
12. Describe what you did the first time you sexually abused him or her.
13. Had you planned to sexually abuse the child on that occasion?
14. What were you thinking before the abuse started?

15. What were you feeling before the abuse started?

16. Describe your state of sexual arousal.

17. What were you thinking during the sexual abuse?

18. What were you feeling during the sexual abuse?

19. What were you thinking immediately afterwards?

20. What were you feeling immediately afterwards?

21. Tell me what you said to the child during the sexual abuse.

22. What did you think the next day?

23. How did you feel the next day?

24. How did you ensure that the child told no one?

25. Why did you abuse him or her again?

26. Did the method of your abuse change, did you perform different sexual acts on the child, did you get the child to perform different acts on you?

27. Did the child ever ask you to stop?

28. If so, what did you do?

29. How long did the sexual abuse last? (once, months, years)

30. How did you ensure that you were alone each time you sexually abused him or her?

31. How do you feel now about what you did to that child?

Case study

John's sexual offending behaviour

Allegations re six-year-old boy when John was 17 years old

John was initially reluctant to talk about this because 'nothing had been proved and it never went to court'.

When asked to describe the circumstances surrounding the allegations, John said that he had met him at Paul R's house. He could not remember the boy's name. He was the younger brother of one of the teenagers who regularly visited Paul R. He was very cheeky for his age and would mimic the behaviour of the older children, who sometimes made fun of him. This made him angry.

He said he was not fat, not thin, not tall but not small either. He said he was not attracted to him in any way.

According to John, the boy accused him of inappropriate touching when they were playing; he would tickle the boy all over his body, including his 'willy'. He would also make the boy touch him 'on his privates'. John denied doing any of these things although he said he might have touched the boy accidentally when he was playing with him. The boy also alleged John had masturbated while he had his hand inside the boy's trousers. John said the boy might have seen him masturbating, something he did a lot when he was a teenager, but that he always did this in the privacy of his bedroom. The boy did, however, have a habit of walking into his bedroom uninvited.

He denied having any sexual feelings in respect of the boy; he had not done anything to him so he had nothing to feel guilty about.

Sexual abuse of Adel

John said Adel was Rachel's daughter and nothing to do with him (biologically). She was seven years of age and he had started to live with Rachel before Adel was born. He said that he never had 'that bond with her, probably because she is not mine'.

He said she was advanced for her years; she already had the first sign of breasts and was quite tall for her age. He described her in the following terms:

'She is a stroppy little cow.'

'I have to make her do things all the time.'

'She is always complaining.'

'She has to be made to go to school.'

'She is thick at school.'

'She really winds me up – she does it on purpose.'

'Rachel has no control over her at all.'

'She has always been jealous of me and her mother.'

'She has always wanted to split us up, to have her mother all to herself.'

'Sometimes she makes me so angry.'

John confirmed that on one occasion he had digitally penetrated Adel. He sometimes bathed her when she was small and continued to do so from time to time as she got older and when he was in the mood. He said he never intended to do anything to her but she was being awkward and he started tickling her to make her laugh. He wanted her to enjoy being bathed. She was giggling and 'her arms and legs were all over the place'. The tickling continued as he was drying her. John said he was shocked when he realised that he had an erection; he said Adel noticed it and started giggling really loudly. She turned away from him and bent over. He saw her vagina and 'just out of interest really I stuck my finger in'. As soon as he realised what he had done he removed his finger. He denied any form of sexual gratification from the episode. Adel said nothing. He continued to bathe her after that but never repeated the abuse.

He said the next day he did not feel guilty as 'it was a sort of accident really'.

According to John, no further episodes of abuse have occurred.

John was reminded that the court had made a 'Finding of Fact' and that the medical evidence indicated that the sexual abuse had been persistent and Adel's disclosure included allegations of vaginal and anal penetration. John denied that he had 'ever done anything like that to her'. He became very angry and the interview was suspended to give him the opportunity to recover his composure. He continued to deny these specific allegations.

It was pointed out to John that children of Adel's age would not usually make allegations such as these unless they were true. John replied that she had never liked him and had always resented the fact that her mother always preferred to be with him than her daughter. He said that Adel's 'lies' were her way of getting back at him. He said she had been determined to split the family up.

John was unable to say why Adel showed substantial signs of sexual abuse. He could not think of anyone who had the opportunity to abuse her but he could not say for sure. He said she had a habit of putting things inside herself and said this is how the injuries had probably occurred.

He said that he 'hated' Adel for trying to break up the family and for being responsible for him being forced to leave the family home. He said he felt very angry with Adel because of her lies. He said when things got back to normal, when they were back to being a 'family', he would sort her out.

Issues arising from this information

- Denial and minimisation is apparent.

- Anger featured in the abuse.

- Opportunity was evident.

- There is evidence of blurred sexual boundaries in the Paul R household.

- He has a negative concept of Adel. She makes him feel angry, there are issues of jealousy and he probably feels she is a rival to his relationship with Rachel.

- Aspects of anger-motivated intra-familial abuse are apparent.

- John's explanation is at odds with the medical evidence and suggests minimisation and denial.

- His ongoing anger towards Adel is of concern.

2.18 VICTIM EMPATHY

Understanding the adult's empathy towards children who have been sexually abused and specifically the victim(s) of the adult's abuse enables the practitioner to:

- gain some understanding of the process of the abuse

- understand the dynamics which may have been in operation at the time

- evaluate the adult's potential to engage in a treatment programme

- design appropriate child protection plans

- enable the child and family to go forward either together or separately.

It will also give further understanding about the adult's cognitive distortions, how they operated at the time and whether they are still in place.

Addressing victim empathy has two aspects:

- The first is to look at empathy in respect of the sexual abuse of children generally.

- The second focuses specifically on the sexually abused child.

Checklist for the adult's victim empathy

1. How do you feel about children who have been sexually abused?

2. Do you think they should be helped to overcome the abuse?

3. How do you think the child felt physically when you sexually abused him or her?

4. How do you think the child felt emotionally when you sexually abused him or her?

5. How do you think she or he will feel now physically?

6. How do you think she or he will feel now emotionally?

7. Did the child ever ask you to stop sexually abusing them?

8. If so, did it bother you?

9. Does it bother you now?

10. How do you feel now about what happened?

Case study

John's responses to the checklist on victim empathy

John began this session by re-stating that he was not a pervert, that he had only inappropriately touched Adel once and he had learned his lesson and would not do anything like that again.

He thought that sexual abuse was wrong if children were hurt by it but that 'sometimes it does them no harm'.

He said that some girls were sexually active with other boys of their age so what was the difference. Some girls deserved it because they 'asked for it' because of what they said and did.

In respect of Adel he said that:

'She has not really been sexually abused, like being raped or anything like that.'

'She has already got over it.'

'She is bragging about having sex with other kids since she went into care, so it can't have done her any harm.'

'It has not done her any physical damage.'

'She is not emotionally damaged in any way, ask her, she will tell you.'

John was reminded that the paediatric evidence suggested that Adel had been sexually abused over a long period and the court had agreed with that. He said that 'Someone else must have done it then.'

When asked how that made him feel he replied, 'She seems okay. If someone else has abused her they should be done for it.'

John denied that Adel had ever asked him to stop abusing her because it had only happened once.

Issues arising from the information

- There is no evidence of victim empathy and this demonstrates that John's concepts and belief systems remain fundamentally unchanged.

2.19 SUPPORT SYSTEMS

The adult's support systems can be an important feature in enabling them to remain within the family and also to provide protection for the child(ren). Where the abusing adult cannot safely remain within the family support may be available to facilitate any contact arrangements.

Checklist for support systems

1. How many people do you know who support or help you?

2. How many of these people are family?

3. Do you have any friends who are your friends and not your partner's?

4. If so, how often do you see them?

5. Do you feel you have a supportive family?

6. Describe the support/help each of them offers.

7. How often does each of them support you?

8. Do you find you need a lot of help and support?

9. How often do you feel you need support?

10. What other support would you find helpful, for example from professionals?

11. Does anything/anyone get in the way of the support you would like?

Case study

John's responses to the checklist on support systems

John said that he does not have any support from members of his family.

His only external support is from Paul R, who he described as a friend and mentor. 'He is the father I never had.'

John said he had some friends who were not also Rachel's friends. They were people he had met through his friendship with Paul R.

John does not believe he needs any other form of support. He describes the professional involvement as interference and wishes that people would leave him and Rachel alone so that they could get on with their lives.

Issues arising from this information

- John's main support is from Paul R, a known sex offender.

- He is not positive about professional support.

2.20 THE FUTURE

This is the last session with the adult perpetrator. There is a possibility that the assessment process has provoked some movement on the part of the adult. His or her thinking, concepts and belief systems have been challenged by the practitioner and some changes may have occurred. It is therefore important to incorporate into this last session questions which will establish the most current position being adopted by the adult. In the final evaluation of the material collected this information can be compared with that previously collected to establish the extent of any change and how this fits with the 'model of change' (Prochaska and Di Clemente 1982 as cited in Adcock, White and Hollows 1991).

This session can also be used as a macro summary of the issues.

The checklist is designed to address the following issues:

- what the adult would like to happen

- whether that can be accommodated within the context of the risk he or she poses

- what child care and child protection issues need to be considered

- the changes the adult has made

- the need for change and the adult's capacity and desire for change

- the adult's motivation to attend a treatment programme.

Checklist addressing issues of 'the future'

1. Do you think you were a risk to children?

2. If not, why not?

3. If so, in what ways were you a risk?

4. Do you think you are a risk to children now?

5. If so, in what ways are you a risk?

6. How do you think that risk can be managed?

7. What do you want to happen in the future?

8. Do you believe you need to make any changes to achieve what you want to happen?

9. If so, what changes do you think you need to make?

10. Do you think a treatment programme will help you?

Case study

John's answers to the checklist on the future

John said he has never been a risk to children. Apart from the one time when he touched Adel he has never had any interest in children at all. He said that was done on the spur of the moment and he regretted it immediately afterwards. He described himself as a normal person. Because he has not been a danger to children in the past he does not represent a danger to them now.

He was asked about the child pornography he had accessed on the computer and said he had heard Paul R and some others talking about it and was curious. He said he had not used child pornography in any sexual way at all.

He wants to return to live with Rachel and their two children, Stephanie and Jasmine. He insists that he is not a risk to children. When asked about Adel returning home he said:

'She should, so I can sort her out.' (By this he meant manage her difficult behaviour.)

'But she will have to stop lying about me.'

'She is at no risk from me.'

'But I bet she will not want to come home.'

He does not believe he needs to change in any way. He said that he does not need to attend a treatment programme as he is not a risk to children but if professionals feel that is an essential prerequisite for him to return to his family, he will attend one. He did comment that he had attended an anger management course when he was in prison but that was a waste of time.

Issues arising from this information

- John's responses give further evidence that his concepts and belief systems remain unchanged.

- Denial is again evident.

CHAPTER 3

The Non-abusing Adult

3.1 THE NON-ABUSING ADULT

There are times when, despite what has happened, families want to remain together. Although the disclosure of sexual abuse often disintegrates adult relationships and separates families, that is not always the case. The non-abusing or potentially 'safe parent' needs to be assessed specifically to address the following issues:

- to understand the person's background and evaluate how that has informed his or her behaviour

- to understand his or her current thinking, concepts and belief systems

- to understand the extent to which he or she contributed to or collaborated with the abuse

- to explore the level of care and parenting available to the child and other children of the family

- to explore the perpetrator's relationship with his or her partner, and establish whether or not they are able to manage the behaviour of the perpetrator and look after the child in ways which will prevent further sexual abuse.

Even when adults separate the risk of safe care may be an issue, for example if contact is to take place, and it may be necessary to conduct the assessment for those purposes. It is sometimes the case that adults say they have separated because they believe that will enable care to be retained by the 'safe parent' but they continue with the relationship and intend to re-engage at a time in the future when they believe they can do so undetected. The following issues therefore need to be addressed:

- an understanding of the relationship

- the extent to which any separation is likely to be long term.

Possible reactions of the non-abusing adult

The non-abusing adult may have very different reactions to the disclosure of sexual abuse by the child. Some adults may have had their suspicions, others may have, to a greater or lesser extent, colluded with the abuse. For some adults it will be a complete shock and surprise.

Practitioners will need to take account of these possible reactions, for example, how recent they are, within the context of the assessment.

Understanding the non-abusing parent's reaction will form part of the assessment. These reactions may include:

Denial of sexual abuse

This is a frequently encountered response. The adult may deny that such abuse could have occurred and may try to convince professionals that is the case. Disclosures of sexual abuse present the non-offending parent with the potential destruction of their relationship/marriage and the disintegration of their family. Some adults cannot imagine that the abuse has occurred. 'I would have known if something was happening, he/she would have told me', is a typical comment.

Rationalisation

Examples of this might be:

> My husband is a nice man.
>
> He is just a very affectionate father.

Minimisation

Examples of this might be:

> It only happened once or twice.
>
> It was only fondling, it could have been much worse.
>
> It wasn't sexual, he or she was only being affectionate.

Defensiveness

For some parents the disclosure of sexual abuse makes them feel that they have done something wrong, missed something or not been sufficiently diligent on child care matters. Some adults will want to tell others that they had no role in the abuse and that they are good parents. They may need reassurance about their parenting skills, if that is appropriate.

Guilt

Others will feel guilty that they did not recognise signals given to them by the child or the physical signs of sexual abuse. Comments might include:

> I feel terrible – how could this have happened?

Ambivalence

Guilt can make adults behave in an ambivalent manner but this should not be seen as a lack of concern for the child or the allegations.

Sadness/depression

This will be conveyed by flatness, lack of expression and a low general mood. Some adults will have accessed medical help to deal with the impact of what has happened.

Fear

Some adults respond with a fear/concern that further abuse may occur and their attitude towards the child is not then one which would be seen as a 'normal' part of their parenting style.

Anger

This may be seen as the projection of feelings directly related to the abuse or a fear response because of the uncertainty of what lies ahead in the future. Sometimes the anger is directed inappropriately and indiscriminately; at other times it is focused on specific people or situations, for example, when contact with the adult perpetrator is occurring.

3.2 ASSESSING THE NON-ABUSING ADULT
Venue for the assessment sessions

The principle must always be that the interview should take place where the adult feels most comfortable and relaxed. This is often in the family home and if that is the appropriate venue the practitioner should facilitate that. However, practitioners may want to consider a different venue, where for example, the adult perpetrator continues to be a member of the household or where interviews at home reinforce issues, for example fear, anger.

It is preferable for such interviews to be solely with the non-abusing adult. If however the interviews can be more appropriately facilitated by a supporter being present and that does not compromise the information in any way, consideration should be given for this. This may particularly be the case where the non-abusing adult has any level of learning disability.

The abusing adult should not be present during any of the interviews. When interviews are being conducted at a neutral venue the abusing adult should not, if at all possible, accompany the non-abusing adult to the session.

The information collected from the interviews uses the same checklists as for the abusing adult up to and including the *Checklist for the sexual abuse of children*. Thereafter specific checklists dedicated to the non-abusing adult are included with the other checklists. Those additional checklists follow in this section. The original checklists are not repeated but should be used in the same sequence.

Case study

Rachel's family

Rachel's mother is Joan. She is 39 years old and lives in a residential home for adults with a learning disability and mental health problems. Rachel used to visit her mother every week but Joan no longer recognises her and would become angry and upset when Rachel visited. Their last contact was two years ago, although Rachel phones the residential home from time to time to see how she is.

She does not know her birth father.

Her mother's former partner was Alan F. Since his release from prison for the sexual abuse of Rachel he has moved away from the area. Rachel does not know his current whereabouts.

She has two full siblings.

- Sheila is 26 years of age and lives with her partner and two children in Scotland. They have no contact and Rachel commented, 'She disowned me when I told them what my dad [Alan F] had done to me, she said I was lying.'

- Her brother Jason is 25 years of age. He suffers from autism and lives with adult carers. Rachel visits him every month and described their relationship as good.

Rachel's chronology

Rachel was brought up by her mother for much of her early childhood. There were child protection concerns because of neglect and Rachel was admitted to care on a number of occasions because of her mother's admissions to psychiatric hospital. The majority of these episodes were with the same carers and Rachel remembers this as a happy period in her childhood.

When she was eight years of age, Alan F joined the family as her mother's partner. From the age of 9 to 14 she was sexually abused by Alan F. She said that she told her mother when it first started but was beaten and called a liar. She never told anyone after that as she did not think she would be believed. The abuse stopped when she became pregnant and named him as the father. He was subsequently sentenced to eight years in prison.

She met John at a drop in centre when she was pregnant with Adel.

They have two children, Stephanie, aged five and Jasmine, aged three.

Since the children were removed by the local authority Rachel has lived at the family home. She sees John every day.

Rachel's experiences from childhood and in adult life

Her mother did not work during Rachel's childhood and according to Rachel she spent most of the time visiting friends and neighbours when she was at home. She also spent periods of time in the local psychiatric hospital. Rachel described her in the following terms:

'She used to drink a lot.'

'She used to shout a lot.'

'She said she never wanted me, I was an accident, a mistake – she said if she had found out about me sooner she would have had an abortion.'

'I had to stay off school sometimes to look after Jason because my mother used to lose her temper with him and hit him.'

'She was poorly a lot and could not look after us properly.'

'When she was well she was okay.'

'When she was poorly she would hit all of us, sometimes for doing nothing.'

'I know it wasn't her fault she was ill but she could have looked after us better.'

Rachel felt her mother's most positive feature was that she laughed a lot when she was well. She least liked her mother when she was ill, when she was drinking and when she lost her temper. She was angry with her mother because she did not believe her when she reported the sexual abuse by Alan F.

Rachel said that she had seen her mother and stepfather having sex a number of times, usually in the evening when they had been drinking. She recalled several occasions when her mother was screaming for him to stop. At the time she did not understand why but now thinks it was because her mother did not want to have sex. I asked if she thought her mother was therefore being raped and Rachel agreed that might have been the case. Rachel's mother once said to her that she hated sex but had to put up with it because that's how you keep men happy.

Her stepfather worked as a security guard at a local factory, often working nights. During the day he was in bed and they had to remain very quiet. If they made too much noise he would hit them. She always felt that Sheila was his favourite because she was always being bought things and was allowed to remain up much later than Jason and her. Rachel described him in the following terms:

'He was usually in a bad mood.'

'He was different when people visited – he was all nice and friendly.'

'After he came to live with us, the house was tidier – he made us clean it from top to bottom every Saturday before we could go out and play.'

'He was nice sometimes – he would take us out to the seaside in the summer.'

'He liked a drink but I have never seen him drunk.'

'He said I was stupid because my reading and writing was not too good.'

'I tried to do things to make him like me but he never did.'

Rachel felt the thing she most liked about him was that before he lived with them her mother was lonely. She least liked the sexual abuse.

In respect of the sexual abuse, Rachel said that it started when she was nine years old. She was usually first in from school and he would walk into her room when she was changing into her play clothes. Sometimes he would play fight with her and touch her. This progressed to him putting her hand on his penis, first with his trousers on and then naked. If she was late in from school he would send her to her bedroom for the whole evening. She told her mother the first time she was made to touch his penis but was not believed. By the time she was ten years old she was either masturbating him or providing oral sex. She thinks she was raped by him just before her twelfth birthday and at least weekly thereafter until she became pregnant at the age of 14.

She does not believe that either of her siblings was sexually abused.

When it was pointed out to Rachel that the preferential treatment that her sister Sheila received is typical of the abuse process she accepted that it was possible she had been sexually abused but if she was Rachel did not know anything about it.

She thinks she was abused and not her sister because Sheila was more confident than her. She said, 'Our Sheila would have sorted him out if he had tried anything with her.'

At the time she was being abused, Rachel felt helpless to do anything about it, especially after she had told her mother and was beaten. At times she was angry and sometimes she cried but he seemed to enjoy it when she cried and so she made herself stop. She used to cut herself and this made her feel better.

When she looks back on the abuse she feels angry. Sometimes she can remember exactly what happened and at other times it is a vague memory.

Rachel had some counselling when she first went into care but she did not feel able to continue with it after Adel was born. At present she does not feel counselling would do her any good. She has talked to John about what happened to her but he said it was one of those things and she should forget it.

Rachel feels she would have been happier if she had not been abused but that her life would have turned out the same as it is now.

She remembered happier times when she was living with Mr and Mrs M, her foster carers. Mrs M would tell her stories before bedtime and cuddle her, something her mother never did.

At school Rachel had difficulty. She missed some school because she had to remain at home to look after her brother, Jason. When she was at school she was bullied by other children because her clothes were usually dirty and ill fitting. She had difficulties with her reading and writing and was called names such as 'stupid' and 'thick head'. She told her teachers but nothing was done to prevent the bullying. She was told to stop complaining all the time. Rachel had one close friend but this relationship ended when her family moved to another town. Rachel was nine years old at the time.

She saw her childhood as being 90 per cent bad and 10 per cent good. The good memories were when she was living with the foster carers. Bad memories included the sexual abuse she suffered, being beaten, not being cuddled and feeling less well treated than her siblings. She learned the following lessons:

'Not to hit my children.'

'To give them lots of cuddles.'

'To be nice to people.'

'Not to argue with people when the children are around.'

'To be a family, we were never a family.'

Issues arising from this information

- Rachel's childhood was abusive and neglectful. She is likely to have felt frightened and emotionally insecure.

- She was subjected to physical and emotional abuse.

- She was sexually abused and was not believed by her mother.

- Her daughter Adel is the result of sexual abuse where she was the victim.

- She witnessed inappropriate sexual activity between her parents and may have been influenced by her mother's concept of a sexual relationship.

- Rachel did not receive counselling and does not appear to be keen on such therapy.

- The abuse and bullying at school indicate a vulnerable, exploited youngster.

Case study

Rachel's perception of self

Rachel sees herself as a sad person who would like to be happy but does not know how she will achieve that. She is usually shy and prefers to remain at home rather than go out. She does not have many friends and feels that John is her best friend as well as her partner. She used to have some friends before she met John, mainly people she had met when she lived with her foster carers, but John said they were only being friendly so that they could take advantage of her.

She described herself in the following terms:

'I spend a lot of time at home.'

'I don't like being by myself.'

'I find it difficult to get to know people.'

'I am shy when I don't know people.'

'When I get to know people I can be more noisy with them.'

'I love my children.'

'I love John, he takes care of me.'

'I think I should be more confident, but I find that difficult.'

'I think I am a good mother.'

'I still have difficulty with my reading and writing – John reads things for me when they come in the post.'

In response to specific questions she replied:

'I still get picked on by people.'

'Sometimes I lend neighbours things and they don't return them.'

'People around here owe me money I have given them – I don't expect I will get it back.'

'John says I am too soft – he says that people take advantage of me.'

The thing she most likes about herself is that she has three beautiful children. The thing she least likes is that she feels sad most of the time.

She is happy when she sees the children, when John is in a good mood and when she visits her brother Jason. Her happiest memories include the birth of her children, when she was living with foster carers and when she first met John. When she is happy she can become really excited and John has told her that she acts in a very childish manner which he does not like.

She is sad when she leaves her children after contact, when John is angry with her and when people pick on her. When John brings his friends round and they make fun of her she feels sad. Her saddest memories are when she was sexually abused as a child and when the children were taken into care. She was extremely sad when the social workers said she had to leave the foster home with Adel and move into a flat. She is sad for the majority of the time at present but believes that if the children are returned and John can come home she will be happy.

She has never seen herself as an expressively angry person although sometimes she feels 'angry inside'. These feelings are present when she has been picked on by other people or when people make her do things she does not want to do. For example John makes her do sexual things when his friends visit which she does not like. He also stops her going out when she wants. Her most angry feelings involve thinking about the abuse she suffered as a child and the time when her children were removed. When she is angry she becomes upset and cries. The angry feelings she has remain with her most of the time and sometimes she self-harms to 'let things out'. This includes cutting her arms and biting herself.

Rachel has been seen by a psychiatrist and psychologist. Psychiatric input has occurred at times when she has self-harmed and for a period when she was about 14 years old and living with foster carers. She was having nightmares at the time about the abuse she had suffered. Educational psychologists were involved because of difficulties she had at school and she received some counselling as a teenager from a psychologist.

She does not think she is sexually attractive to the opposite sex because she is fat. John has told her she will never find another man because she is fat, ugly and sexless.

She does not want to be sexually attractive to other women. She has never felt sexual feelings for her own sex.

She does not believe she has any sexually attractive features.

She thinks that sex should only happen when you are in love with someone. She has never, of her own choice, had sex with people she did not love. Her only sexual partner of choice has been John. She and John have sex about every day and she thinks that is too often. She said she prefers conventional sex but John likes oral sex and sometimes he makes her have anal sex. She really does not like this and it hurts her but John insists. She has seen pornographic films and there are 'loads in the house'. She has never used it as an aid to sex but John often does.

She has never seen any child pornography and has never accessed any Internet sites but she is aware that John has been accused of that and his computer has recently been taken by the police.

Issues arising from this information

- The report suggests a shy person with a low level of self-confidence.

- She is socially isolated and relies on John to look after her. A significant level of dependency is seen. This is a contra-indicator to her ability to protect the children from John.

- She is a vulnerable adult who will be prone to exploitation in the future.

- John demands sexual activity with Rachel with which she clearly disagrees. This gives evidence of the dominant/submissive nature of their relationship.

- John reinforces Rachel's poor image of herself.

Case study

Rachel's association with other adults

Re Paul R

Rachel has known Paul R since she was 15 years of age. She met him through John. She said he was kind and gave them a room in his house so they could be together.

She said there had never been a physical or sexual relationship between them although he had tried to kiss her a few times when she first moved into his house. She had let him touch her breasts once when he told her she should be grateful that he had given them somewhere to live. She often found him staring at her during those early years and felt uncomfortable with him when John was not around. He had not shown any interest in her in recent years.

She described him in the following terms:

'He can be nice.'

'He can be nasty.'

'He is more nasty to women than to men.'

'John thinks he is great – he does what Paul says most of the time.'

'He has hit me a few times when I have made him angry.'

'They say he has messed about with girls.'

When this last comment was further explored Rachel said she did not believe that he has committed the offences for which he was convicted. When asked why she thought that, she replied that John had told her he was innocent.

I asked Rachel what she thought and she said she thought the girls had been lying about what Paul R had done to them. When asked why she thought they would lie about such a thing she said she did not really know.

Rachel thinks that some of his friends have been accused of doing things to children. She was unclear as to whether or not this was physical abuse or sexual abuse.

Rachel said she does not think that Paul R or any of his friends are a risk to Adel or her other two children. John has told her they are not a risk and she trusts John's judgement.

Issues arising from this information

- Paul R has been physically abusive towards Rachel and has in the past made sexual advances towards her.

- She accepts John's perception that he has not sexually abused children and she would not therefore be alert to his behaviour and/or in a position to protect her children.

Case study

Rachel's perception of John

Rachel described John in the following terms:

'He looks after me.'

'He says that without him I would not be able to manage.'

'He says I am too daft to look after myself.'

'He is nice if I do as he tells me.'

'He can get angry if I have done something wrong.'

'It's my fault when he gets angry because I have done something to upset him.'

'He can be kind sometimes.'

'He does not get on with Adel, he gets very angry with her when she does not do as she is told… It is her fault when John gets angry with her.'

'He gets angry with Stephanie sometimes – he says she is getting like Adel.'

The thing she most likes about John is that he looks after her. She likes him least when he is angry with her.

She described their relationship as good. John has physically hurt her, 'but not that often and only when I have made him angry'.

Rachel was asked why she felt it was her fault when John hit her and she replied, 'John has said so, and so has Paul R…and I do make him angry when I forget things, or forget to do things.'

If she could change anything about John it would be his temper and his anger. She said she would not want to change anything else and said that John was an ideal partner who loved her and the children. She wanted them to be together as one happy family.

Issues arising from this information

- This confirms her dependency on John and her inability to act independently of him. Her ability to protect the children is therefore compromised.

- John's attitude towards Stephanie, 'she is getting like Adel', is a worrying feature.

Case study

Rachel's perception of her children

Adel

Adel is Rachel's child. Her father was Rachel's mother's former partner who sexually abused Rachel. Rachel looked after Adel until she made the disclosure of sexual abuse against John. She is currently placed with foster carers.

She said that she had difficulties with her as a baby, because she was uncertain and nervous, but John showed her what to do and her parenting was okay.

As her daughter has got older she has had more difficulty in managing her. Adel has become more cheeky and demanding and this has led to arguments. Rachel does not feel able to manage her and John often has to take over when Adel is in one of her moods.

When asked whether she thought Adel always told the truth she replied, 'I thought so until she told these lies about John.'

Adel had been to the doctor a number of times for various things. She had been treated for anal warts about one year previously.

She said that Adel did not like doing as she was told and would have tantrums when she could not get her own way.

She does not believe that Adel has been sexually abused by John. When it was put to her that there was evidence of sexual abuse she was unable to say how or when that could have happened. She said she thought Adel had lied about the abuse because she was jealous of John.

She thinks that Adel would describe her as 'soft'. She feels Adel believes she can get her own way with her.

Stephanie

Stephanie is the daughter of Rachel and John. Rachel looked after Stephanie until she was removed following the discovery that her parents were meeting in breach of the child protection agreement.

Rachel said that Stephanie was a good baby who slept through the night and fed well.

She described Stephanie in the following terms:

'She is bright.'

'She does as she is told most of the time.'

'Lately she has become defiant – like Adel, John has started to get angry with her sometimes.'

'She can be jealous and possessive.'

'She does not get on with Adel.'

When Stephanie is in a bad mood she does not listen to her mother and sometimes argues with her father.

She said that Stephanie has definitely not been abused. When asked how she knew she said that she just knew.

Jasmine

Jasmine is three years old; she is the daughter of Rachel and John. Rachel described her in the following terms:

'She does as she is told.'

'We have had no problems with her at all.'

According to Rachel, Jasmine is meeting her milestones and developing well. They are delighted with her progress. She has not been referred to a doctor or hospital for any medical examination or treatment.

Issues arising from this information

- Rachel perceives Adel as a daughter she is unable to control and cannot manage.

- She does not believe her daughter and this compromises her ability to protect her. She has clearly adopted John's view on this matter.

- She supports John's view about Stephanie and this also compromises her ability to protect her second daughter.

- There are no reported concerns in respect of Jasmine.

Case study

Rachel's criminal history

Rachel has no criminal convictions or matters currently before the court.

Rachel's responses to the checklist on drugs and alcohol

Rachel reported that she has used alcohol since she was a teenager. She would drink as often as possible and commented that being drunk helped her to forget the abuse she was suffering.

Since she has had the children she has used alcohol less frequently, sometimes becoming tipsy and on the odd occasion drunk.

She does not drink now because John does not like it and she knows that he would become angry with her if she had too much to drink.

She has never tried any form of illegal drugs. She is afraid of the effect. She knows that John would be angry with her if he found out she had been taking any drugs.

Issues arising from this information

- No concerns are raised. However, more evidence is provided regarding the influence John exercises over Rachel.

Case study

Rachel's self-esteem

Rachel's self-esteem is very poor. She does not have a good concept of herself physically, finds it difficult to interact in novel social situations and does not have confidence in her skills, abilities and competence.

Issues arising from this information

- Adults with poor self-esteem are likely to feel less confident, less able to challenge or assert themselves and their ability to protect themselves and those for whom they have responsibility is not usually good.

Case study

Rachel's response to the checklist on dominant/submissive behaviour

Rachel does not see herself as a confident person. She tends to feel most confident when she is with John as he makes the decisions for both of them and she trusts him.

She does not like to be in control of situations as this makes her feel stressed.

She would not argue if she thought she was right about something and tries to avoid arguments whenever possible. She might try to make her point but not always and accepts that sometimes she gives in to other people in order to avoid an argument.

She can be nervous a lot of the time and believes she is more nervous than most people. She is not stubborn, does not usually get her own way and said that John makes all of their important decisions. She tries not to show her emotions but sometimes she bursts into tears if she is upset.

Issues arising from this information

- Rachel's passive compliant behaviour is very apparent from this checklist.

- She is dominated by John, would not act against his wishes and relies upon his guidance at all times.

- She shows no ability to protect herself or her children.

- She is vulnerable to exploitation.

Case study

Rachel's responses to the angry, aggressive and violent behaviour checklists

Rachel said she is not an angry person; she feels sadness more than any other emotion. She does not lose her temper, except sometimes with herself when she has done something wrong.

Rachel said she has never been violent to anyone. The most violent thing she has ever done was to smash a cup when she was a teenager. She could not remember the circumstances.

She has never been violent to another person and has never felt the need to be violent.

She has never wanted to hurt anyone, not even the person who sexually abused her. She has many times in the past thought about hurting herself and self-harmed several times as a teenager. She sometimes has those same thoughts since the children were removed from her care.

She avoided fights and disputes as she was growing up, never bullied anyone and sees herself as less violent than other people.

Issues arising from this information

- There is no evidence of violence and Rachel is likely to be less violent and angry than most other people.

- Angry feelings are internalised and professionals should be alert to any signs of self-harming behaviour.

Case study

Rachel's responses to the checklist on the sexual abuse of children

Rachel believes that the sexual abuse of children is anything which hurts them and involves their 'private parts'. She said that 'private parts' was 'their bottom and vagina'. She was uncertain whether or not a child's bust was a sexual area. Rachel was asked what she meant by 'hurts them'. She said that if they were upset afterwards then it was abuse. It was put to Rachel that some sexual abuse involved children being made to touch adults and that would not physically hurt them but would be sexually abusive behaviour. She appeared to be unsure about this comment.

Rachel was asked if she had ever discussed the sexual abuse of children with anyone. She said she and John had talked about it after Adel had made her disclosure. When asked if they had ever spoken about it before then she said they had from time to time. I asked who had raised the subject. She replied that John had always raised the subject, mainly when he had been drinking.

'He had talked about it not hurting kids, he had known loads of kids who had been abused and none of them had been affected.'

'He said that if it did not hurt them it was not wrong.'

When asked how she felt about these comments she replied that it made her confused.

Rachel thinks it is wrong to sexually abuse children. She was abused and it hurt her considerably.

Rachel said that when children get older they should be allowed to decide for themselves whether or not they want to have sex. She was unable to qualify what she meant by 'older', but commented that some of the girls she had seen visiting Paul R were old enough to agree to sex.

Rachel feels the age of sexual consent should come down because 'teenagers are doing it all the time with each other'. When asked whether teenagers should be allowed to consent to sex with adults much older than themselves she said it was okay if the teenagers were not hurt.

Rachel was referred once more to her own childhood and said that was different because she did not want it to happen.

Rachel said she had not thought about a lot of the issues which were discussed in respect of the age of consent and the differences of gender and sexual abuse. She has listened a lot to what John has had to say about such matters and agrees with him. She is happy that he advises her about such things.

Issues arising from this information

- There is evidence that Rachel's view on sexual abuse is confused and at times contradictory.

- Much of what she says is clearly influenced by John's view on these matters.

- Her comments raise significant concerns about her concepts and belief systems and are a clear contra-indicator to her ability to protect her children from sexual abuse.

Case study

Rachel's responses to the checklist for victim empathy

Rachel said that she still loves her daughter Adel and wants to look after her. She does not, however, believe that she has been sexually abused by John and is upset that Adel has said the things about John.

She does not know why her daughter should lie about such a thing.

Rachel was asked how she would feel if she discovered that Adel had been sexually abused but not by John. She said she would be upset and would want the person prosecuted.

She was asked how she would feel if, for example, she said she had been sexually abused by Paul R. Rachel said she would not believe that as he would not do anything to Adel.

Asked what her view was on the medical evidence and court judgement supporting the sexual abuse disclosure of Adel she said that John has told her she could have done things to herself to get him into trouble or hurt herself playing. She thinks that is what she has done.

Issues arising from this information

- There is no empathy shown by Rachel towards her daughter, despite her own experiences of being sexually abused as a child.

- Rachel's dependency on John is further confirmed.

- Her attitude towards Adel is very worrying.

Case study

Rachel's responses to the checklist on support systems

Rachel has no contact with her family. She said she would like to see them from time to time but John does not like them and says she cannot see them.

She said she has no friends of her own.

The main support she receives is from John and she relies on him 'for everything'.

She enjoys it when the social worker comes and would like that to happen more often but she knows John would be against that. Sometimes she feels lonely and would like to join some clubs or groups but John will not let her.

Issues arising from this information

- Rachel has no positive support systems and is isolated from potential support by John.

3.3 ABILITY TO PROTECT

In order for the non-abusing parent to be able to protect the child(ren) an understanding must be gained of their ability to do so. Practitioners may want to revisit some of the answers given in the checklists already administered, and may therefore not need to use all of the questions asked in the following dedicated checklist.

An understanding of the non-abusing parent's understanding of the grooming process is essential both to evaluate immediate risk and perhaps to identify possible training or familiarisation programmes.

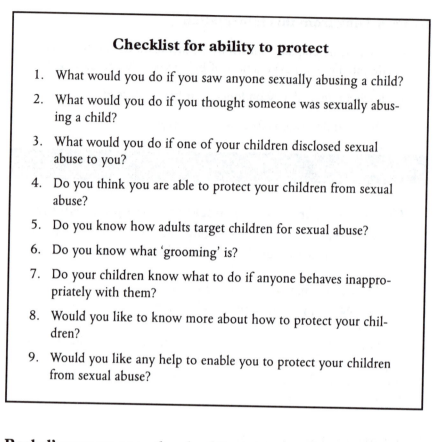

Checklist for ability to protect

1. What would you do if you saw anyone sexually abusing a child?

2. What would you do if you thought someone was sexually abusing a child?

3. What would you do if one of your children disclosed sexual abuse to you?

4. Do you think you are able to protect your children from sexual abuse?

5. Do you know how adults target children for sexual abuse?

6. Do you know what 'grooming' is?

7. Do your children know what to do if anyone behaves inappropriately with them?

8. Would you like to know more about how to protect your children?

9. Would you like any help to enable you to protect your children from sexual abuse?

Rachel's responses to the checklist on protecting children

Rachel feels she is able to protect her children from sexual abuse. Because she was abused as a child she thinks that she would be able to tell if that was happening to any of her children.

If any of the children made a disclosure to her she would tell John immediately and he would know what to do.

When asked what she would do if one of the children said that John had sexually abused them she initially said that he would not do that to one of the girls and then added that she would ask John if they should tell the social workers.

She thinks that she might need some help in understanding what happens to children when they are sexually abused and what kind of things to look for. She said she thought John might help her as he understands such things better than she does.

She said she would like to be more confident and has been told about courses on assertiveness which she would like to attend although she has spoken to John about this and he has said he does not want her to do anything like that. He has said to her that as long as he is around he will make sure nothing happens to her or the children.

Issues arising from this information

- All of the indications are that Rachel would not have the ability to protect her children.

- She would not be alert to any signals of abuse they might give.

- She would always give John the benefit of the doubt and believe his version of events.

3.4 THE FUTURE

For the non-abusing adult, the disclosure could well have come as a complete shock and surprise. In some cases, some suspicion may have existed and in others a knowledge that the child(ren) were being sexually abused.

Denial may have been the non-abusing adult's initial presentation. With some adults that may have remained and even been reinforced by the perpetrator's continued ability to manipulate, dominate or reconstruct matters in their favour. With some non-abusing adults there may have been an increasing realisation of the truth and a determination to establish a non-abusive environment for the child(ren).

Practitioners must realise that the child's disclosure, any subsequent child protection actions and this assessment could have challenged established concepts and belief systems, dismantled relationships and families and caused significant physical and emotional trauma. Account should be taken of this.

It is important to determine the non-abusing adult's intentions and preferred future arrangements as well as seeking to establish how they would respond to the actions and decisions of professionals and the court.

Rachel's responses to the checklist on the future

Rachel said she wanted the children returned to her care and John to come home to live.

If she ever saw John doing anything to the children she would be upset and would tell someone but she knows that will never happen as he loves the girls.

Checklist addressing issues for 'the future'

1. What would you like to happen now?

2. Do you believe that your partner presents a risk to children?

3. Do you believe anyone else presents a risk to children?

4. Do you think you understand those risks?

5. Do you think you can manage those risks?

6. If yes, how would you do that?

7. Do you feel you will need support to manage any risks?

8. If yes, what support do you think you will need?

9. Will you receive support from any family and/or friends?

10. If yes, what will that support be?

11. What will you do if professionals believe you should separate from your partner?

12. What will you do if professionals believe it is not safe to return the children to your care even if you say you will separate from your partner?

13. What would you like to be happening in your life in one, three, five and ten years' time?

She is aware that professionals have said Paul R is a risk to children. Although she does not believe that to be the case she will ask John not to remain friends with him and not to allow him to visit their home. She is afraid however that this would make John angry.

She was asked what she would do if John refused to do this and she replied that she thought John would do anything to be able to live together as a family.

Rachel could not imagine being without John and if this was a requirement for the children to be returned to her care she said, 'I can't manage without John, if it was a choice between him and the children I don't know what I would do…but they can't make me do that because John has not done anything to Adel.'

Rachel wants to be living with John and the children until the children grow up and leave home and then she wants to remain with John. She commented, 'I don't know what I would do without him…he looks after me…he takes care of me.'

Issues arising from this information

- Rachel is unlikely to disconnect from John.

- Her dependency on him is significant as is his influence over her.

- She continues to see him as being no risk to the children.

- She is afraid of John's anger.

3.5 EVALUATING THE INFORMATION

Collecting the information in the systematic way provided within this book is the foundation for the assessment of adults who sexually abuse children and of the non-abusing adult.

Evaluating and interpreting that information then enables an understanding of the risk the adult poses and the ability of the non-abusing adult to safeguard and promote the welfare of the child(ren).

Research, the findings of Enquiry Reports and Social Services Inspectorate inspections have frequently highlighted weaknesses in this area of assessment. A great deal of time and effort goes into the information gathering stage. This results in an assessment that focuses on describing what is happening. However, often less attention is given to the analysis of the information gathered. (Department of Health 2000, p.10.)

The evaluation in respect of the abusing adult relies upon:

- an assessment of the person through an understanding of their history and how that informs current behaviour and relationships

- the adult's chronology, childhood and life experiences and how those have been internalised

- the adult's behaviour and how that impacts upon relationships, in particular the relationship with the child(ren) and the non-abusing adult, and also issues of power and control

- the offending behaviour

- the cycle of abuse used by the adult

- the adult's current concepts and belief systems in respect of sexual abuse

- an understanding of any changes the adult has made since the abuse occurred and during the assessment and the adult's capacity to change and the desire to do so.

The evaluation in respect of the non-abusing adult relies upon:

- an assessment of the person through an understanding of their history and how that informs current behaviour and relationships

- the adult's chronology, childhood and life experiences and how those have been internalised

- the adult's ability to protect

- the dynamics within the relationship between the abusing adult and non-abusing adult

- their understanding of the risk posed by the perpetrator

- the adult's understanding of the sexual abuse cycle and specifically the cycle used by the abusing adult

- the adult's ability to access appropriate support systems

- an evaluation of the adult's capacity for change, to develop new skills and the desire to do so.

The abusing adult

Presentation and behaviour

The information from the checklists 'Perception of self', 'Criminal history – non-sexual offences', 'Drugs and alcohol', 'Self-esteem', 'Dominant and submissive behaviour' and 'Angry, aggressive and violent behaviour' all contribute to this part of the assessment. They do not, however, 'stand alone'. The practitioner will have gained valuable information through observation and discussion, for example the adult's body language, demeanour and overall/specific attitude. Information collected within other checklists may also contribute to the evaluation within this phase of the assessment.

Assessment checklist for presentation and behaviour

1. How did the person present during the assessment?

2. Which sessions, if any, were difficult?

3. What was the level of co-operation?

4. Was the co-operation different from that seen in other assessments? If so, why?

5. Were any special arrangements needed, for example interpreter, supporter, etc.?

6. What level of competence does he or she have? Comments should be confined to known assessments by professionals, for example psychiatrists or psychologists.

7. How was account taken of levels of competence, for example the use of limited language in the case of a person with learning difficulty or the use of specific assessment material?

8. How was the adult's mood: good, poor, low, variable?

9. Was the person's mood consistent or did particular sessions have an impact on mood?

10. What was the person's overall presentation? Within what range of behaviour was the person usually seen? Was the person passive, submissive, assertive, dominant, hostile, aggressive, and what does this mean in terms of:

   • their general behaviour

   • their relationship ability and capacity

   • their child care abilities, including child protection?

11. Did the person respond with different behaviour in different situations, and what does this mean in terms of:

   • their ability to manage

   • their relationship ability and capacity

   • their child care ability and capacity?

12. Did the person respond with different behaviour when relating or responding to different people and what does this mean in terms of:

    • their ability to manage

    • their relationship ability and capacity

    • their child care ability and capacity?

13. Within the range of overall presentation, what other aspects of behaviour were evident and what is the effect of this?

14. Is anything known about the person's mental health?

15. Is anything known about the person through psychological assessment?

16. Is there any other expert opinion about the person?

17. Is there any significant medical information about the person which has an impact on the person's life?

18. Do drugs, alcohol or solvent abuse have a significant impact on the person's life?

19. If drugs, alcohol or solvents are an issue, how and under what circumstances are they used? For example are they a part of normal life or are they used in response to stress?

20. Do they act as a disinhibitor to behaviour?

21. Do drugs, alcohol or solvents lead to angry or violent behaviour?

22. Are there any significant issues of anger or violence?

23. At what level is the person's self-esteem?

24. What information comes from the checklists which have been completed?

25. How well does the person manage within the community? Are particular strategies used and how successful are these?

26. Describe the person's social network.

27. Describe the person's network of personal, interpersonal and social arrangements.

28. Does the person require external support systems to sustain them in the community?

29. Are the person's current social, personal and interpersonal arrangements likely to continue? If so, why?

30. What is the significant behaviour of the person and how does this impact on their ability to function?

31. Describe any negative or positive indicators which would impact on the ability to safeguard and promote the welfare of children.

Experiences from childhood and in adult life

The person's experiences in childhood and adult life and the way those experiences have been internalised will inform their behaviour, concepts and belief systems.

An abusive childhood is likely to have left the adult feeling fearful, isolated and lacking in self-confidence. Their ability to form purposeful adult relationships may have been compromised and could affect their ability to safeguard and promote the welfare of children.

Conversely, positive and safe childhood experiences enable children to explore their world with confidence, establish good peer group relationships and feel emotionally secure. In adult life they are more confident and are likely to establish secure attachment arrangements with their own children.

Assessment checklist for experiences from childhood and in adult life

1. Describe the overall arrangements of childhood care. For example was the person brought up exclusively by parents, were the arrangements varied, were there any episodes in care?

2. What was the person's perception of each parent?

3. What was the relationship with each parent?

4. What was the relationship with any significant others?

5. What are relationships like now?

6. What relationship did the person have with siblings?

7. What is that relationship like now?

8. What is the evidence of good care, love, appropriate affection, nurturing or other positive emotional experiences?

9. What is the evidence of rejection, isolation, loneliness, abandonment, or any other negative experiences?

10. What was the likely level of attachment?

11. Are there any childhood experiences which are likely to have caused significant harm or which indicated unsafe care?

12. Describe the relationship between his or her parents.

13. Were any parenting strategies abusive?

14. Were the behaviour management strategies positive or negative?

15. If the child was physically, emotionally or sexually abused in childhood, how has that affected them?

16. If the child was abused has any form of help been offered?

17. If so, what is the consequence of that help?

18. Are the person's childhood experiences positive or negative?

19. How has the person internalised those experiences? For example, being hit as a child may lead to the use of similar systems or a determination not to hit children.

20. Do the person's childhood experiences have a significant impact on current behaviour?

21. Are there any unresolved issues from childhood which have an impact on the person's emotional wellbeing, ability to function or ability as a parent?

22. Are the person's perceptions of childhood realistic? If not, how does this impact on their view of parenting?

23. What have been the person's experiences in adult life?

24. Have any child protection concerns been raised in respect of their care of children?

25. If so does this influence the issue of child sexual abuse?

26. Describe their level of competence in adult life.

The relationship between the abusing adult and the non-abusing adult and the relationship between the adult and other significant adults

The evaluation of these relationships will determine:

- whether the abusing adult can be a member of the household

- whether the non-abusing adult is able to protect the children

- what contact arrangements are possible and the role of each adult in that

- whether other relationships present a risk

- whether other relationships enable the risk to be reduced or managed.

Assessment of the relationship between the abusing adult and the non-abusing adult and the relationship between the adult and other significant adults

1. Describe the relationship.

2. What are the positive elements of the relationship?

3. What elements of the relationship present a risk to children?

4. What elements of the relationship present a sexual abuse risk to the children?

5. Which adult is dominant within the relationship?

6. If so, is that to an extent that safe care systems can be put in place?

7. If the abusing parent is dominant within the relationship, what is the extent of risk which that poses to the children?

8. Is the relationship capable of change?

9. What is the extent of relationship change which will be required in order to ensure the ongoing sexual health of the child(ren)?

10. If the adults are required to live apart will the non-abusing adult be able to facilitate and appropriately supervise any contact which is envisaged?

The adult's concept of children

How the adult perceives children, how the children of the family and how the child victim is perceived can be evaluated from the description they give of them in the checklists 'Perception of children of the family', 'Adult's concepts about sexual abuse', 'The sexual abuse of the child' and 'Victim empathy'.

Assessment of the information re the concept of children

1. What is the adult's general view of children?

2. Are particular children favoured?

3. Are particular children less well favoured?

4. Are particular children targeted?

5. Evaluate the relationship between the adult and the children of the 'family'.

6. Was any empathy towards the children evident?

7. Evaluate the relationship between the adult and the child(ren) who were sexually abused.

8. How does the adult manage the behaviour of the child(ren) of the 'family' and the child who was sexually abused?

9. Are there any child protection concerns other than the sexual abuse?

Assessing the information re sexual abuse

The assessment should address the risk which the adult abuser poses and this risk falls into two categories.

Static factors

Static risk factors are fixed and based upon previous history and known information. Hanson and Harris (1998) identified the following static features:

- sexual interest in children

- any deviant sexual preference

- prior sex offences

- failure to complete treatment

- any personality disorder

- negative relationship with mother

- victim was a stranger

- antisocial personality disorder

- preference for boys

- has prior criminal offences

- has anger problems

- offender is older than 23 years

- early onset of offending

- victim was a male child

- diverse sex crimes.

Dynamic risk factors

Dynamic risk factors are those which are not fixed and must be evaluated within the context of each unique case. There are two branches to dynamic risk factors.

1. Stable dynamic factors

   Hanson and Harris (2003) identified the following:

   - significant social influences

   - intimacy deficits

     o lovers/intimate partners

     o emotional identification with children

     o hostility towards women

     o general social rejection/loneliness

     o lack of concern for others

- sexual self-regulation
  - sex drive/preoccupation
  - sex as a coping mechanism
  - deviant sexual interest
- attitudes supportive of sexual assault
  - sexual entitlement
  - rape attitudes
  - child molester attitudes
- co-operation with supervision
- general self-regulation
  - impulsive acts
  - poor cognitive problem-solving skills
  - negative emotionality/hostility.

2. Acute dynamic factors

   Hanson and Harris (2003) identified the following:

   - victim access
   - emotional collapse
   - collapse of social supports
   - hostility
   - substance abuse
   - sexual preoccupations
   - rejection of supervision.

In addition there are a number of issues which have a positive impact upon the assessment. Veeder, Brake and Tanner (1999) describe these as *measures of willingness*.

- Sees self as ongoing risk.
- Makes successful disclosure (polygraph).

- Minimises contact with potential victims.

- Admits abuse and discusses details.

- Shows little or no manipulation.

- Has engaged significant others in containment circle.

- Keeps no secrets from group or therapist.

- Seeks confrontation on own behaviour.

- More concerned with errors than proving no errors.

- Is limiting in own lifestyle.

- Confronts others in treatment group.

- Completes all treatment assignments.

- Initiates development and utilisation of 'safety plans'.

- Has continued successful maintenance polygraphs.

- Uses covert tapes.

- Uses other tools (maintenance and reinforcement) frequently.

- Demonstrates empathy for victims and potential victims.

- Shows suppression of deviant arousal behaviour.

The information collected from the checklists 'Adult's concepts about sexual abuse', 'The sexual abuse of the children', 'Victim empathy' and 'The future' should all be used in this part of the evaluation, alongside the practitioner's observations and notes from other parts of the assessment. (The 'issues arising from this information' notes at the end of each checklist are an example of the possible interpretation of the information for the evaluation.)

It is recommended that the practitioner uses the *risk factors* and *measures of willingness* to form an opinion in respect of the risk or otherwise the abusing adult presents to the sexual abuse of children. Each of the issues identified represents a potential risk or potential positive; the accumulation of the positives and negatives enables the practitioner to form a view as to the danger the abusing adult represents to children.

Evaluating denial and minimisation

The issue of denial will form part of the assessment of risk, but also it is helpful for practitioners to understand the type of denial or minimisation which is occurring as this may assist with subsequent treatment programmes or support/monitoring arrangements.

Many abusing adults either maintain denial throughout the assessment or minimise their behaviour.

- Denial tends to prevent an understanding of the cycle of abuse. However, there may be compelling reasons why the abusing adult will maintain this position. Admission risks destroying the adult relationship, would normally lead to a prison sentence and denies the abusing adult access to children. In some cases the revulsion felt by the abusing adult results in 'blocking' the ability to admit what they have done. Genuine and sincere remorse may lead to admission but may also lead to the need to continue denying what they have done.

- Minimisation may be used to justify or excuse the behaviour. In some cases it is used as a tool to convince the non-abusing adult of their 'innocence'.

Marshall, Anderson and Fernandez (1999) identify features of denial and minimisation which practitioners may find helpful in identifying the category into which the abusing adult fits.

- Complete denial

  False accusation:

  'The police are out to get me.'

  'The victim hates me.'

  'The victim's mother is using it to deny me access or get back at me.'

  Wrong person:

  'It must have been someone else.'

  Memory loss:

  'I'm not like that so I doubt that it happened.'

  'It could have happened but I can't remember.'

- Partial denial

  It was not really sexual abuse:

  'The victim consented.'

  'The victim enjoyed it.'

  'She was a prostitute or promiscuous.'

  'The victim said she or he was older.'

  'I was only massaging him or her.'

  'I was putting cream on his or her genitals.'

  'It was only play.'

  'It was love.'

  'It was educational.'

  Denial of a problem:

  'I did it but I am not a sex offender.'

  'I will never do it again.'

  'I don't have an interest in kids or forced sex.'

  'I don't have deviant fantasies.'

- Minimising the offence

  'It was less often than the victim says.'

  'There was no coercion/force/threats.'

  'The intrusiveness was less than the victim claims.'

  'There are no other victims.'

- Minimising responsibility

  'The victim was seductive/provocative.'

  'The victim's parents were neglectful.'

  'I was intoxicated.'

  'I was stressed/emotionally disturbed.'

  'My partner was not sexually satisfactory.'

  'I have a high sex drive.'

  'The victim said no but meant yes.'

- Denying/minimising harm

  'People tell me the victim was not harmed.'

  'The victim's current problems were not caused by me.'

  'I was loving and affectionate so could not have caused harm.'

  'I was not forceful so could not have caused harm.'

- Denying/minimising planning

  'I acted on the spur of the moment.'

  'Things just unfolded.'

  'The victim started it.'

- Denying/minimising fantasies

  'I do not have deviant sexual fantasies.'

  'I did not think about abusing the victim prior to the actual offence.'

Checklist for assessing the risk presented by the abusing adult

1. Are the adult's concepts and belief systems identified as those which promote the sexual abuse of children or do they indicate 'safe' thinking and belief systems?

2. Give examples as evidence of your opinion.

3. Has the adult created a family/environment/involvement which enables sexual abuse to occur or where safe care can take place?

4. Give examples as evidence of your opinion.

5. Are there any static factors which indicate risks are evident?

6. Are there any dynamic risk factors evident?

7. What positive steps has the abusing adult taken to minimise the risk they present?

8. Are these steps consolidated and will they stand the test of time?

9. What is your view about these steps?

10. Are they sufficient to develop a safe caring environment for the child(ren)?

11. To what extent is the adult denying or minimising the abuse.

12. Identify the type of denial and minimisation being used.

13. Are you able to identify the cycle of abuse?

14. If so, describe it.

15. Are you able to identify the grooming process?

16. If so, describe it.

The future

This part of the assessment can be completed using the dedicated checklist. Practitioners should be seeking to evaluate how the future plans of the adults will impact upon the risk of sexual abuse which the intended arrangements are likely to have.

The non-abusing adult

The practitioner must first of all be reassured that no other child protection concerns have been raised by other professionals or are evident during the assessment. If they have, checklists which are available in 'A Practitioner's Tool for Child Protection and the Assessment of Parents' (Fowler 2003) should be used to address those concerns.

Browne and Herbert (1999) identified those characteristics relating to women who could possibly be groomed by adults who are targeting children for whom they have responsibility. These characteristics include:

- low self-esteem
- feelings of inadequacy
- social isolation
- poor social support
- poor assertiveness skills

- a history of minor psychiatric disorder such as anxiety or depression

- compliant behaviour.

Practitioners should be looking for these characteristics when assessing the non-abusing adult as they represent contra-indicators to the ability to safeguard and protect the welfare of the child(ren).

Assessing the information re sexual abuse and the ability to protect

1. What is the adult's view on the sexual abuse of children?

2. Does the non-abusing adult believe that the child has been abused by the abusing adult?

3. If not, why not?

4. Does the non-abusing adult have the ability to protect child(ren) generally from abuse and exploitation?

5. If not, why not?

6. Is the adult able to protect the child(ren) from sexual abuse by the abusing adult?

7. If not, why not?

8. Are there a range of services/support/interventions which will allow the non-abusing adult to protect the child(ren) from sexual abuse?

9. If not, why not?

10. If yes, is there a timescale involved in developing appropriate skills to protect the child(ren)?

11. Are there any relationship issues to be resolved following the disclosure of the sexual abuse?

12. If the adult has care of the children, will he or she be able to manage any contact arrangements in ways which will safeguard and promote the welfare of the child(ren)?

The evaluation of the information in respect of the non-abusing adult uses the same evaluation checklists as those used with the abusing adult:

'Presentation and behaviour'

'Experiences from childhood and in adult life'

'Adult relationships'

'The children'

'Issues of sexual abuse'

'The future'.

A crucial element is the non-abusing adult's general level of assertiveness and the dynamics which exist in the relationship with the abusing adult. If the non-abusing adult is submissive within that relationship, unable to resist the impositions of the abusing adult or is manipulated by them, then their ability to safeguard and promote the welfare of the child(ren) is likely to be compromised. The evaluation uses the same questions as are addressed in the section on the abusing adult.

The non-abusing adult's answers on the issues of sexual abuse must look specifically to the issues of safe care and protection. It requires an evaluation of the adult's ability to protect the child(ren) from the abusing adult.

The case study: conclusion

The case study has been designed to show clearly the high risk which John presents in terms of the sexual abuse of children. There is substantial evidence of this from the information collected.

Equally it demonstrates that Rachel is not able to protect the children from the risk which John presents. There is also substantial information to evidence this.

TERMS AND TOOLS USED IN ASSESSING ADULTS WHO SEXUALLY ABUSE CHILDREN

Although most of these tools and guides are used for adults who have been convicted of sex offences and are based upon a forensic model, practitioners may find them helpful in assessment work. They should never be relied upon as stand alone assessments of adults who sexually abuse children. Some are based upon index offences and account should be taken of that.

Their value is in supporting the assessment process rather than informing it.

Community-Sex Offender Group Programme (C-SOGP)

Such programmes are designed to help adults convicted of contact or non-contact sex offences. The aim of the work is to prevent further sexual re-offending by looking at how thoughts, attitudes and emotional responses are linked to the offending behaviour. It usually allows adults who have denied or minimised their offending behaviour to participate.

Sex Offender Treatment Programmes (SOTP)

Sex Offender Treatment Programmes are designed to help prevent adults from re-offending. They typically use:

- *cognitive-behavioural approach*, which emphasises changing patterns of thinking that are related to sexual offending and changing deviant patterns of arousal

- *psycho-educational approach*, which stresses increasing the offender's concern for the victim and recognition of responsibility for their offence

- *pharmacological approach*, which is based upon the use of medication to reduce sexual arousal.

Static 99

This is a risk assessment for sex offenders developed by Hanson (Department of the Social General of Canada, Ottawa) and Thornton (Her Majesty's Prison Service, London) (Hanson and Thornton 2000). It identifies potential risk factors and the score on each is applied to a grid which labels the risk the adult represents on a scale from low to high.

Rapid Risk Assessment for Sex Offender Recidivism (RRASOR; Hanson 1997)

The RRASOR was designed to predict sex offence recidivism using a small number of easily scored variables:

- prior sex offences

- any unrelated victims

- any male victims

- aged between 18–24.99 years.

Structured Anchored Clinical Judgement (SAJC; Graham 2000)

The SAJC aims to predict sexual and violent recidivism using a staged approach, with each stage incorporating different types of information.

- The first stage incorporates the adult's official convictions.

- The second incorporates eight potentially aggravating factors.

- The final stage applies only if the adult has entered a treatment programme.

Sex Offender Risk Appraisal Guide (SORAG; Quincey *et al.* 1998)

The SORAG is used to assess the risk of violent recidivism of previously convicted sex offenders.

Sexual Violence Risk-20 (SVR-20; Boer *et al.* 1997)

This is a 20-item guide for assessing risk in sex offenders.

Sex Offender Need Assessment Rating (SONAR; Hanson and Harris 1998)

The SONAR includes five relatively stable risk factors: intimacy deficits, negative social influences, attitudes tolerant of sex offending, sexual self-regulation, general self-regulation and four acute risk factors: substance misuse, negative mood, anger and victim access.

The levels of risk of harm used by Offender Assessment System (OASys)

- *Low*: no significant current indicators of risk of harm.

- *Medium*: there are identifiable indicators of risk of harm. The offender has the potential to cause harm but is unlikely to do so unless there is a change in circumstances, for example failure to take medication, loss of accommodation, relationship breakdown, drug or alcohol misuse.

- *High*: there are identifiable indicators of risk of serious harm. The potential event could happen at any time and the impact would be serious.

- *Very high*: there is an imminent risk of serious harm. The potential event is more likely than not to happen imminently and the impact would be serious.

Multi-agency Public Protection Arrangements (MAPPA)

MAPPAs consist of professionals and agencies in dedicated areas who have responsibility to establish the arrangements for public protection, including the protection of children from sexual abuse.

REFERENCES

Adcock, M., White, R. and Hollows, A. (eds) (1991) *Significant Harm*. London: Significant Publications.

Allen, C.M. (1991) *Women and Men Who Sexually Abuse Children. A Comparative Analysis*. Orwell, VT: Safer Society Press.

Bagley, C. and King, K. (eds) (1990) *Child Sexual Abuse, The Search for Healing*. London: Routledge.

Beckett, R., Beech, A., Fisher, D. and Fordham, A.S. (1994) *Community Based Treatment for Sex Offenders: An Evaluation of Seven Treatment Programmes*. London: Home Office Publications Unit.

Boer, D.P., Hart, S.D., Kropp, P.R. and Webster, C.D. (1997) *Manual for the Sexual Violence Risk – 20. Professional Guidelines for Assessing Risk of Sexual Violence*. Burnaby, BC: Mental Health, Law, and Policy Institute, Simon Fraser University.

Bolen, R.N. (2001) *Child Sexual Abuse: Its Scope in Our Failure*. New York: Plenum.

Browne, K. and Herbert, M. (1999) *Preventing Family Violence*. Chichester: Wiley.

Buss, D.M. and Schmitt, D.P. (1993) 'Sexual strategies theory.' *Psychological Review 100*, 204–232.

Cooper, C.L., Murphy, W.D. and Haynes, M.R. (1999) 'Characteristics of abused and non abused adolescent sex offenders'. *Sexual Abuse. A Journal of Research and Treatment 8*, 105–109.

Department of Health (1992) *Memorandum of Good Practice (on Video-recorded Interviews with Child Witnesses for Criminal Proceedings)*. London: The Stationery Office.

Department of Health (2000) *Framework for the Assessment of Children in Need and their Families*. London: The Stationery Office.

Department of Health (2006) *Working Together to Safeguard Children: A Guide to Inter Agency Working to Safeguard and Promote the Welfare of Children*. London: The Stationery Office.

Department for Constitutional Affairs (2003) *Protocol for Judicial Case Management in Public Law Children Act Cases*. Accessed on 18 December 2007 at www.hmcourts-service.gov.uk/docs/protocol-complete.pdf

Faller, K.C. (1988) *Child Sexual Abuse An Interdisciplinary Manual for Diagnosis, Case Management and Treatment*. New York: Columbia University Press.

Finklehor, D (1984) *Child Sexual Abuse. New Theory and Research*. New York: The Free Press.

Finklehor, D. (1986) *A Source Book on Child Sexual Abuse*. Beverly Hills, CA: Sage Publications.

Finklehor, D. (1994) 'The victimisation of children in a developmental perspective.' Paper presented at the International Congress on Child Abuse, Kuala Lumpur.

Fowler, J. (2003) *A Practitioner's Tool for Child Protection and the Assessment of Parents*. London: Jessica Kingsley Publishers.

Freel, M. (1992) *Women Who Sexually Abuse Children*. London: Karnac.

Graham, W. (2000) 'Uncovering and eliminating child pornography rings on the Internet.' *The Law Review of Michigan State University – Detroit College of Law 2*, 457–484.

Grubin, D. (1998) 'Sex offending against children: understanding the risk.' *Police Research Series, Paper 99*. London: Home Office.

Hanson, R.K. (1997) *The Development of a Brief Actuarial Risk Scale for Sex Offence Recidivism*. Ottawa, ON: Department of the Solicitor General of Canada.

Hanson, R.K. and Harris, A.J.R. (1998) *Dynamic Predictors of Sexual Recidivism*. Ottawa, ON: Department of the Solicitor General of Canada.

Hanson, R.K. and Harris, A.J.R. (2003) *The Sex Offender Needs Assessment. A Method for Measuring Change in Risk Levels*. Ottawa, ON: Department of the Solicitor General of Canada.

Hanson, R.K. and Thornton, D. (2000) 'Improving risk assessments for sex offenders. A comparison of three actuarial scales.' *Law and Human Behaviour 24*, 119–136.

Krone, T. (2004) 'A typology of internet child pornography offending.' *Trends in Crime and Criminal Justice 279*.

Marshall, W.L. (ed.) (2006) *Treating Sex Offenders. An integrated approach*. London: Routledge.

Marshall, W.L., Anderson, D. and Fernandez, Y.M. (1999) *Cognitive Behaviour Treatment of Sex Offenders*. Chichester: Wiley.

Matthews, J.K., Matthews, R. and Speltz, K. (1989) 'Female sex offenders, a typology.' In M.Q. Patton (ed.) *Family Sexual Abuse. Frontline Research and Evaluation*. New York: Guilford Press.

McCarty, L.M. (1986) 'Mother-child incest. Characteristics of the offender.' *Child Welfare 5*, 447–458.

Quincey, V.L., Harris, G.T., Rice, M.E. and Cormier, C.A. (1998) *Treatment of Sex Offenders, The Handbook of Crime and Punishment*. New York: Oxford University Press.

Sedlak, A.J. and Broadhurst, D.D. (1996) *Third National Incidence Study of Child Abuse and Neglect*. US Department of Health and Human services.

Summit, R.C. (1983) The Child Sexual Abuse Accommodation Syndrome. *Child Abuse and Neglect 7*, 177–192.

Symons, D. (1979) The Evolution of Human Sexuality. New York: Oxford University Press.

Veeder, G., Brake, S. and Tanner, J. (1999) *Measures of Willingness, Sex Offender Assessment Checklist*. Boulder, CO: KB Solutions.

Wolfe, S. (1985) 'A multifactor model of deviant sexuality.' Paper presented at the Third International Conference of Victimology, Lisbon.

FURTHER READING

Becker, J. and Murphy, W. (1998) 'What we know and don't know about assessing and treating sex offenders.' *Psychology, Public Policy and Law 4*, 116–137.

Bentovim, A. (2002) 'Preventing sexually abused young people from becoming abusers, and treating the victimisation experiences of young people who offend sexually.' In D. Briggs, P. Doyle, T. Gooch and R. Kennington (eds) *Assessing Men Who Sexually Abuse. A Practice Guide*. London: Jessica Kingsley Publishers.

Faller, K.C. (1990) *Understanding Child Maltreatment*. London: Sage Publications.

Fisher, D. and Thornton, D. (1993) 'Assessing risk of re offending in sex offenders.' *Journal of Mental Health 2*, 105–117.

Freel, M. (1995) *Women Who Sexually Abuse Children*. Hull: University of Hull.

Freel, M. (2003) 'Child sexual abuse and the male monopoly: an empirical exploration of gender and a sexual interest in children.' *British Journal of Social Work 33*, 481–498.

Hanson, R.K. and Busserie, M.T. (1998) *Predictors of Sex Offender Recidivism*. Ottawa, ON: Department of the Solicitor General of Canada.

Home Office (2003) *MAPPA Guidance Multi Agency Public Protection Arrangements*. London: National Probation Directorate.

Jones, D.P.H and Ramchandani, P. (1999) *Child Sexual Abuse, Informing Practice from Research*. Oxford: Radcliffe Medical Press Ltd.

McCarthy, B.W. (1998) 'Effects of sexual trauma on adult sexuality.' Journal of Sex and Marital Therapy 24, 91–92.

National Commission of Inquiry into the Prevention of Child Abuse (1996) *Childhood Matters. Volumes 1 and 2*. London: The Stationery Office.

Polaschek, D.L.L. (2003) 'Relapse prevention offence process models, and the treatment of sexual offenders.' *Professional Psychology Research and Practice 34*, 4, 361–367.

Quincey, V., Rice, M. and Harris, G. (1995) 'Actuarial prediction of sexual recidivism.' *Journal of Interpersonal Violence 10*, 85–105.

Wolfe, D.A. (1994) 'Factors associated with post traumatic stress disorder among child victims of sexual abuse.' *Child Abuse and Neglect 18*, 1, 37–50.

SUBJECT INDEX

AUTHOR INDEX